Etiquette
for Teens
Grades 6–8+

Author: Schyrlet Cameron
Editor: Mary Dieterich
Proofreaders: Alexis Fey and April Hawkins

ISBN 978-1-62223-919-1

Printing No. CD-405098

Mark Twain Media, Inc., Publishers
Distributed by Carson Dellosa Education

Visit us at www.marktwainpublishing.com

Table of Contents

To the Teacher: Introduction

Etiquette for Teens is designed to help students in grades six through eight and beyond comprehend the basics of polite behavior. Understanding how to act appropriately equips students with the skills necessary to succeed academically and socially.

How the Book Is Organized

Etiquette for Teens encompasses ten units of study: *Etiquette vs. Manners, Social Interactions, Table Manners, Online Etiquette, School Etiquette, Correspondence Etiquette, Family Etiquette, Hygiene, Being a Host or Guest,* and *Showing Respect.* Each of the 23 lessons supports state and national etiquette guidelines. Real-life activities enable students to explore, understand, and practice appropriate behavior in various contexts, including at home, in public, on the phone, and online. This approach fosters meaningful learning and promotes the core principles of etiquette: respect, consideration, and honesty.

Each lesson contains the following sections:

- **Reading Selection:** Introduces students to a specific etiquette rule while building vocabulary.
- **Knowledge Check:** Evaluates student comprehension of information in the reading selection.
- **Knowledge Builder:** Challenging activity that reinforces learning of proper manners and behaviors.

Three Keys of Etiquette

Etiquette vs. Manners

Etiquette and manners go hand in hand. Together, they are a how-to guide on how to behave in different situations. Learning how to behave appropriately provides us with the tools needed to succeed in life.

What Is Etiquette?

Etiquette is a set of rules for how to behave politely in different social situations. Etiquette rules aren't complicated. They promote kindness and being polite. Etiquette includes rules for appropriate behavior in family, school, and social media settings. Following the rules of etiquette helps us to get along with others and to be thoughtful about our conduct.

The main principles of etiquette are:

- **Respect:** caring about how your words and actions may impact others
- **Consideration:** showing kindness and thoughtful concern for others
- **Honesty:** being truthful in what you say and do

What Are Manners?

Manners are polite behavior, such as saying "please" and "thank you," and writing a thank-you note. Good manners are simple: be kind, be respectful, and treat others the way you like to be treated. When you are nice to people, they are likely to be nice to you.

Etiquette vs. Manners

Etiquette is the set of rules for appropriate behaviors, and manners are the behaviors to use in social situations.

Example: Eating

Etiquette (Rule): Be respectful while eating.

Manner (Behavior): Take small bites and keep your mouth closed while chewing food.

Etiquette and Manners Are Good for You

Etiquette and good manners are essential. Being kind, courteous, and considerate shows respect for others, makes them feel appreciated, and helps you build friendships. Learning about proper etiquette and good manners provides you with important skills for a happy and successful life.

History of Etiquette

The history of etiquette can be traced back to the Middle Ages and became formalized at the French royal courts of the 1600s and 1700s. King Louis XIV used etiquette to control the French nobility. He would have cards or signs, called "étiquettes," posted to remind palace visitors of the rules of behavior. The term *etiquette* soon became associated with the rules themselves, and it spread throughout Europe. Today, etiquette guides behavior in social and professional settings throughout the world.

Name: ______________________________ Date: ____________________

Knowledge Check

Matching

_____ 1. etiquette		a. caring how your words and actions may impact others
_____ 2. manners		b. behaviors to use in social situations
_____ 3. behavior		c. conduct
_____ 4. consideration		d. rules for appropriate behavior
_____ 5. respect		e. showing kindness and thoughtful concern for others

Multiple Choice

6. The three principles of etiquette are
   a. caring, concern, consideration.
   b. words, actions, behaviors.
   c. respect, consideration, honesty.
   d. rules, behaviors, actions.

7. An example of respect is
   a. saying "thank you."
   b. learning proper behavior.
   c. knowing the rules of etiquette.
   d. getting along with others.

Did You Know?

In Europe before the 18th century, guests were required to bring their own knife and spoon to a dinner party.

Constructed Response

8. Explain why etiquette and manners are important. Use details from the reading selection to support your answer.

____

____

____

____

____

____

Name: ______________________________ Date: ______________________

Knowledge Builder

Etiquette Vocabulary

Directions: Complete the crossword puzzle. Start by reading the numbered definitions for each word both across and down. Fill in the puzzle grid with the words from the word bank that match the definitions.

Word Bank

etiquette	honesty	rude	social
manners	civility	courteous	attitude
behavior	responsible	rules	apology
appropriate	polite	conduct	proper
consideration	conversation	nice	decorum

Across

2. a person's behavior
6. well-mannered, polite, and respectful
8. proper in the circumstances
9. showing good manners
10. a way of feeling or thinking about something or someone

Down

1. polite behaviors
3. proper and polite behavior
4. a set of rules for polite behavior
5. truthfulness
7. the act of showing respect and consideration for others

Directions: For the ten words from the word bank that were not used in the puzzle above, write a definition for each word on your own paper. Create a crossword puzzle using a free online template. Follow the steps to create and print your puzzle. Trade your puzzle with another student. Solve the crossword puzzle.

Introductions

Learning to give and receive introductions is important. **Introductions** are a formal presentation of one person to another. They are a way to show respect and to help people feel comfortable and part of a group.

Making Introductions to Adults

Introductions consist of two parts. In each part, it is essential to say each person's name to help everyone remember who they are. It's also important to mention how you know the person you are introducing. This clarifies the connection between you and the person being introduced, making it easier for everyone to start a conversation and feel at ease with one another.

- Address a woman first.
  Example: Part 1: "Mrs. Jones, this is my uncle, Mr. Williams."
  Part 2: "Uncle Bill, this is my neighbor, Mrs. Jones."
- Address the older person first.
  Example: Part 1: "Grandpa, this is my friend Tommy."
  Part 2: "Tommy, this is my grandpa Mr. Smith."
- Introduce a person using their title, if they have one.
  Example: Part 1: "Coach Dunn, this is my mom, Susan Long."
  Part 2: "Mom, this is Coach Dunn."
- Introduce your parents to your teacher using the titles Mr. and Mrs. or Miss for the teacher.
  Example: Part 1: "Mrs. Smith, this is my dad, Dan Parnall."
  Part 2: "Dad, this is my science teacher, Mrs. Smith."
- Introduce your friends to your parents using your parents' first names.
  Example: Part 1: "Mom, this is Lisa Hill, my best friend from school."
  Part 2: "Lisa, this is my mom, Anne Smith."

Greeting Adults

Handshakes are often part of the introduction between adults. Stand and make eye contact. Smile and extend your hand to the adult. Using a firm grip and quick handshake, say, "Hi, it's nice to meet you."

If invited to do so, you may call an adult by their first name. If not, address a man as "Mr." and a married woman as "Mrs." or "Ms." Address a single woman as "Ms." Address a married couple as "Mr. and Mrs." For example: Mr. Smith and Mrs. Smith, Ms. Parker.

Introducing Yourself and Friends

If there is a new student at school, walk up to the person and introduce yourself. Smile and say, "Hi, I'm (your first and last name)." They should say their name back to you. If the new friend does not say their name, you may ask, "What is your name?"

When introducing a new friend to a group of your friends, you can introduce everyone at once. Smile and say, "Hi everyone, this is my friend Danny. Danny, these are my friends Tom, Justin, and Larry."

Name: ______________________ Date: ______________

Knowledge Check

Matching

_____ 1. greet
_____ 2. introduction
_____ 3. respect
_____ 4. title
_____ 5. address

a. a word or phrase that comes before or after a person's name to indicate their rank, profession, or status
b. speak to a person
c. caring how your words and actions may impact others
d. welcome
e. a formal presentation of one person to another

Multiple Choice

6. Why is it important to say each person's name twice when making an introduction?
   a. It is the polite thing to do.
   b. It is a show of respect.
   c. It helps everyone remember the new names.
   d. It is their title.
7. Why is it important when making an introduction to include how you know the person you are introducing?
   a. It is fun to learn about people.
   b. It makes it easier to start a conversation.
   c. It is a show of respect.
   d. It is one of the rules of making introductions.

Did You Know?

It is believed the handshake may have originated when early man began to hold out his empty right hand (the weapon hand) as a sign of friendliness and peace.

Constructed Response

8. Explain why learning how to make introductions is important. Use details from the reading selection to support your answer.

____
____
____
____
____
____

Name: ______________________ Date: ______________________

Knowledge Builder

Introducing Yourself and Others

Directions: Complete the two introduction activities.

Introducing Yourself

Step 1: Make eye contact and smile.
Step 2: Greet the person. "Hi, my name is ______."
Step 3: Ask "What is your name?"
Step 4. Reply "It is nice to meet you, (their name)."

Greeting	Reply
Hello Hi Good morning Good afternoon Good evening	It's nice to meet you. Happy to meet you. How do you do?

Activity: John introduces himself to Sam.

John Fields **Sam Whitaker**

Introducing Others

Step 1: Smile and make eye contact with both people.
Step 2: Address a woman, the oldest person, or a person with a title first.
Step 3: Say "(Name of person being addressed), this is (name of person being introduced)." Then repeat with the opposite names. Briefly share relevant details about the people being introduced.

Introduction
This is … Let me introduce you to … I would like you to meet … I'd like you to meet … You haven't met … Do you know …

Activity: Introduce Ann Smith to Jimmy Hill.

____

____

____

____

Making Conversation

Having a conversation is a verbal back-and-forth interaction with others. This is how we get to know people and build friendships. Learning and practicing basic conversation skills will make communicating with others easier.

Conversation Skills

Making conversation is not hard. All it takes is to show interest in what the other person is saying, ask questions, and share your own thoughts.

Example: Smile, make eye contact, and use a friendly greeting. Next, ask a question. Listen to the answer, and then respond with a comment or ask another question.

6 Key Skills

- Initiating a Conversation: Get a conversation started by asking a question. This helps people who don't know each other well to learn common interests before settling on a conversation topic. Topics to avoid include rumors and gossip, people's physical features, and personal details about the lives of others.
- Asking Questions: Questions are very important for having a good conversation, especially when we first meet people or get to know them. Questions help us learn about other people and their interests. The best questions are those with open-ended answers. Some fun things to ask about are sports, hobbies, favorite movies, video games, and music. When we ask people about these things, we can find out what we have in common and maybe make a new friend.
- Listening: By paying attention to what someone has to say, you make them feel good, and you can learn a lot about them. When listening, it is important to sit or stand up straight, look the speaker in the eye, and avoid tapping, squirming, or fidgeting.
- Responding: When someone has finished speaking, you can show you were listening by commenting on what they said or asking a question.
- Taking Turns: It is rude to interrupt while someone is in the middle of a sentence. Wait until they have finished their thoughts, and then you can comment or ask a question.
- Ending a Conversation: Express gratitude for the conversation, give a reason for leaving the conversation, and suggest a future meeting to talk.

Practicing conversation etiquette will make you a better communicator. Developing good conversation skills will help you make friends and develop strong relationships with others.

Name: ______________________ Date: ______________

Knowledge Check

Matching

_____ 1. conversation
_____ 2. verbal
_____ 3. rude
_____ 4. respond
_____ 5. initiate

a. to say something in return
b. a talk between two or more people
c. to start something
d. not being polite
e. spoken

Multiple Choice

6. When someone has finished speaking, you can show you were listening by
   a. shaking their hand.
   b. looking at them.
   c. asking a question.
   d. turning and walking away.
7. The best type of questions to ask during a conversation are
   a. personal questions.
   b. those with open-ended answers.
   c. yes and no questions.
   d. questions about how a person is dressed.

Did You Know?

In ancient Greece, people would often start conversations by discussing the weather.

Constructed Response

8. Explain the purpose of conversation. Use details from the reading selection to support your answer.

____

____

____

____

____

____

Name: ______________________ Date: ______________________

Knowledge Builder

Having a Conversation

Directions: Use the worksheet to practice your conversation skills.

Situation: You are going to your school's first football game of the season.

1. What are some topics that I can talk about with others at the event?

______________________ ______________________

______________________ ______________________

2. What are two things I could say to initiate a conversation?

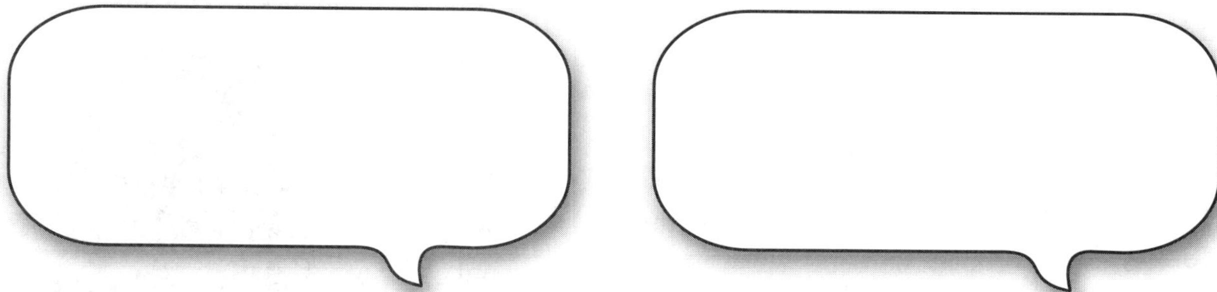

3. What are two questions I could ask to learn about the others and their interests?

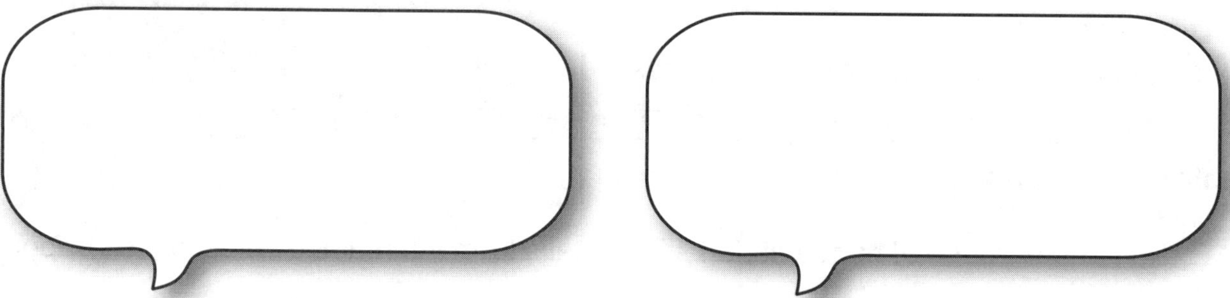

4. What are two things I could say to end the conversation?

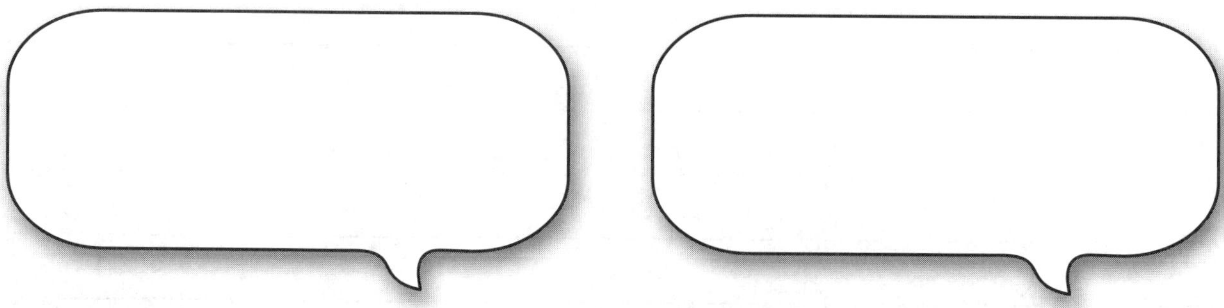

Basic Table Manners

Table manners are basic skills that you will use throughout life. Knowing how to behave appropriately at the table can improve your confidence in social situations, including family dinners, restaurant dining, school lunches, or just hanging out with friends.

Basic Table Manners

Practicing basic table manners can create a friendly and relaxing eating environment for everyone involved. Ten table manners to be used during mealtimes include:

1. Wash your hands with soap and water before a meal. This helps prevent the spread of germs and illness.
2. Sit up straight with both feet on the floor while eating. Do not lean over your plate or put your elbows on the table. Good posture helps your body with digestion!
3. Place the napkin on your lap. Place one hand in your lap with your napkin in it during the meal. Your napkin stays in your lap when you're not using it. The napkin is only for wiping your mouth. It is not polite to blow your nose with a napkin. If you need to leave the table and will be coming back, leave the napkin in your chair. When the meal is over, leave your napkin next to your plate.
4. Eat quietly. Take small bites. This will allow you to close your mouth and chew quietly. While chewing, breathe through your nose. Wait several seconds after swallowing before putting more food in your mouth.
5. Drink quietly. Take sips of your drink without slurping.
6. Politely ask for food to be passed. It isn't polite to reach over the table for something. Don't forget to say "please" and "thank you."
7. Use utensils for eating. Use a fork and knife to cut and eat solid foods. Use a spoon to sip the soup. Hold your fork and spoon similarly to how you'd hold a pencil. Use a fist grip to hold a knife. After taking a bite, you should place your utensils on your plate, not on the table. Place your utensils on the plate when you are finished eating.

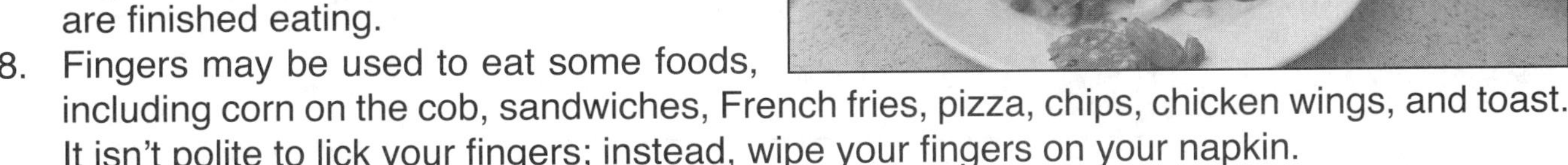

8. Fingers may be used to eat some foods, including corn on the cob, sandwiches, French fries, pizza, chips, chicken wings, and toast. It isn't polite to lick your fingers; instead, wipe your fingers on your napkin.
9. Having no devices at the table will allow you to enjoy the meal while talking to others.
10. Ask permission before leaving the table. Example: "May I be excused?" It is important to say "thank you" before leaving the table to show your appreciation for the time and effort put into cooking the meal.

Gathering around the table and sharing a meal brings us closer together as family, friends, and community. Using proper table manners keeps the experience enjoyable for everyone.

Name: ______________________________ Date: ____________________

Knowledge Check

Matching

____ 1	appreciation	a. breakdown of food
____ 2.	posture	b. a tool
____ 3.	digestion	c. thankfulness
____ 4.	utensil	d. stance
____ 5.	permission	e. approval

Multiple Choice

6. When you have finished eating, place the knife and fork
   a. on the table.
   b. on the napkin.
   c. on the plate.
   d. on your chair.
7. If you leave the table during a meal and will be returning, what should you do with your napkin?
   a. Leave it on the chair.
   b. Place it on the left side of your plate.
   c. Throw it in the garbage.
   d. Take it with you.

Did You Know?

Forks were not in common use in Europe until the 1600s or 1700s. Spoons, knives, or fingers were commonly used when eating.

Constructed Response

8. Explain why table manners are important. Use details from the selection to support your answer.

____

____

____

____

____

____

Name: ______________________ Date: ______________

Knowledge Builder

Manners Table Placemat

Directions: Placemats are usually positioned at each table setting to protect the table from water stains and food spills. Create a colorful placemat for your family. Write an important table manner in each box.

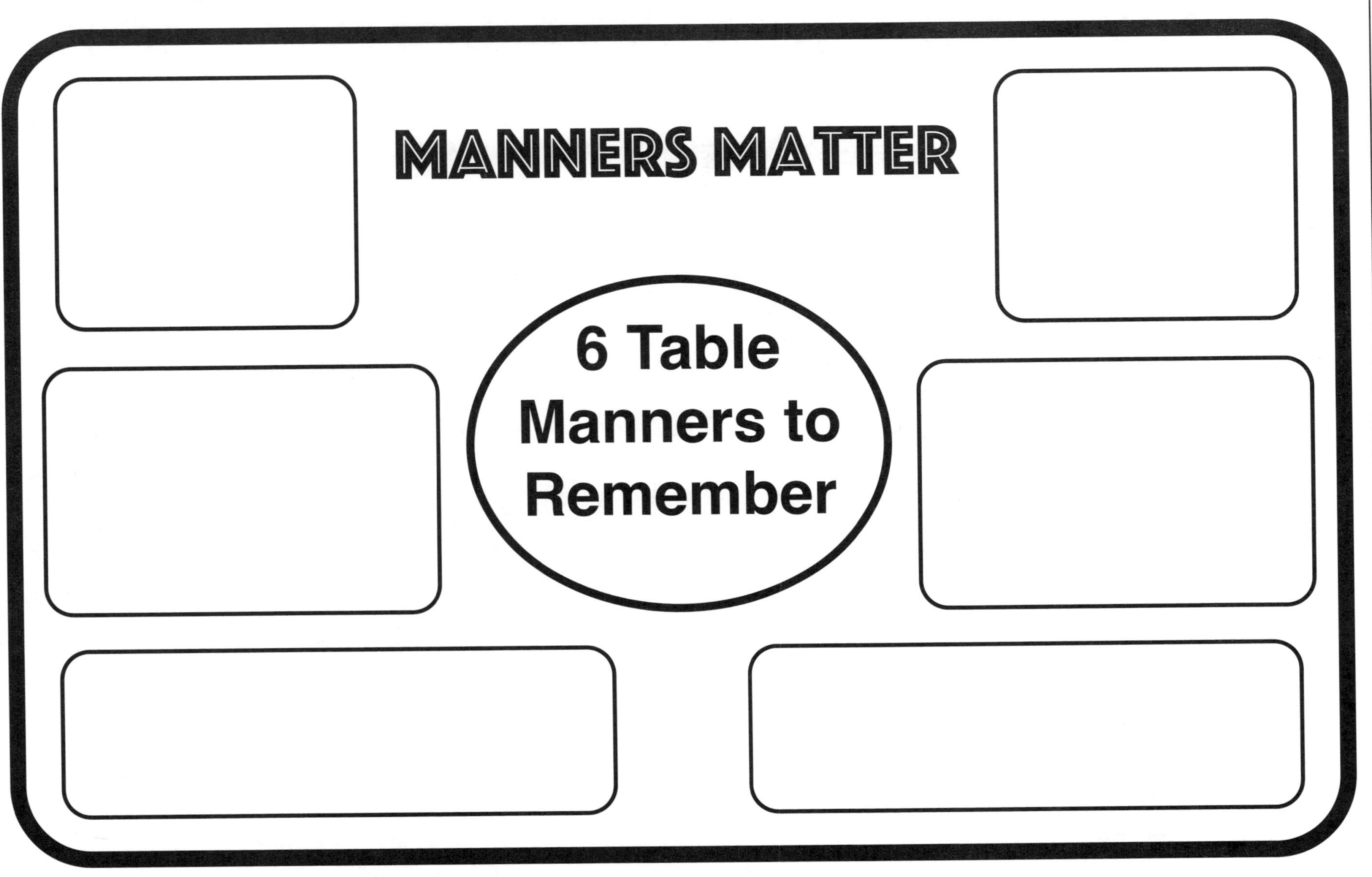

Table Setting

Coming together around the table for mealtimes can be a great family tradition. It gives family members time to share their day and discuss important events and issues. A well-set table can create a more pleasant atmosphere for all involved.

Basic Table Setting

Setting a table is not as difficult as it seems. It is as simple as ensuring each person has a setting placed in front of their seat at the table. Their table setting should have everything they need to enjoy their meal.

Table Setting Rules

- **Placemat:** Lay the placemat down first. It helps protect the table from spills, scratches, and heat from hot plates.
- **Plate:** Place the dinner plate in the center of the placemat. If you are not using a placemat, place the plate on the table where the person will be sitting during the meal.
- **Napkin:** Place the napkin to the left of the plate.
- **Fork:** Place the fork on the napkin. Forks are used with a wide variety of dishes, including pasta, rice, meat, vegetables, and desserts.
- **Knife and Spoon:** Place the knife to the right of the plate, with the knife's blade facing the plate. Place the spoon to the right of the knife. Knives are used for cutting food into smaller pieces. Spoons are used for eating the main course, side dishes, or desserts.
- **Water Glass:** Place the water glass above the knife, to the right of the plate.

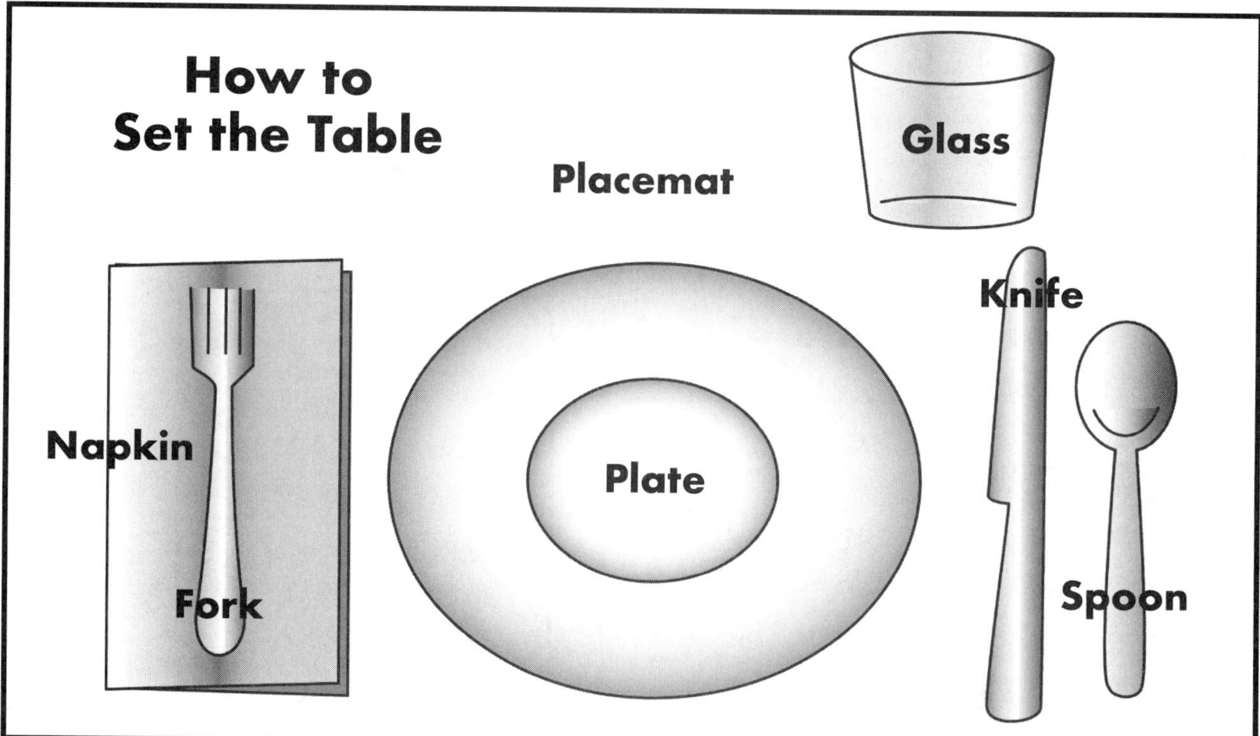

A correctly set table ensures that everything is organized and that everyone has what they need before sitting down to eat, making mealtimes enjoyable for the entire family.

Name: ______________________ Date: ______________

Knowledge Check

Matching

_____ 1. mealtime
_____ 2. knife
_____ 3. table setting
_____ 4. napkin
_____ 5. placemat

a. the arrangement of tableware used for a meal
b. helps protect the table from spills, scratches, and heat from hot plates
c. the usual time for eating a meal
d. used for cutting food into smaller pieces
e. a piece of cloth or paper used to wipe the mouth and hands while eating

Multiple Choice

6. Where is the correct placement of the water glass?
   a. above the fork, to the left of the plate
   b. above the plate, in the center of the placemat
   c. above the knife, to the right of the plate
   d. above the napkin, to left of the plate
7. What is the purpose of setting the table?
   a. to show the cook respect for cooking the meal
   b. to ensure everyone has everything they need to eat the meal
   c. to create a family tradition
   d. to ensure everyone uses the correct utensils

Did You Know?

Forks were not in common use in Europe until the 1600s or 1700s. Some of the first Europeans to use forks were the Italians. They found it useful for eating pasta. Early forks had only two prongs.

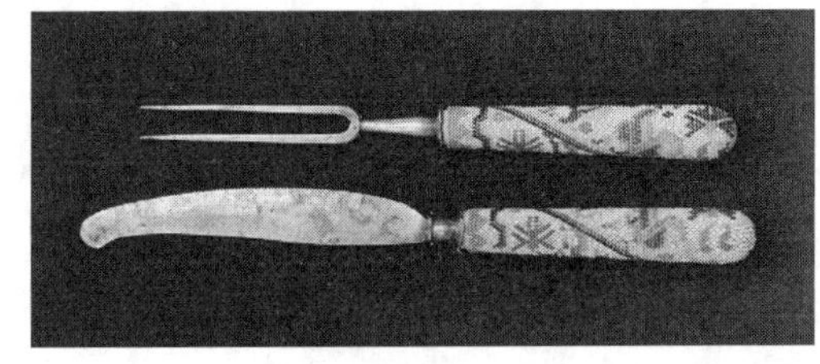

Constructed Response

8. Explain the importance of setting a table correctly. Use details from the selection to support your answer.

____

____

____

____

____

Name: ______________________________ Date: ____________________

Knowledge Builder

Setting the Table

Directions: Name each item and its location on the placemat.

A. ______________________________
____

B. ______________________________
____

C. ______________________________
____

D. ______________________________
____

E. ______________________________
____

F. ______________________________
____

Restaurant Etiquette

Whether having a meal at a buffet bar, fast food restaurant, or a full-service dinner, it is important to remember the basic everyday table manners while using proper dining out behavior. Regardless of the type of restaurant, don't forget to wash your hands and put your phone away.

Guide to Buffet Dining Etiquette

Buffet dining offers a variety of food, and people serve themselves.

- Scan the buffet before you start serving yourself to plan your meal.
- Wait your turn in line and avoid rushing or cutting in front of others.
- Use the provided serving tongs or utensils to get your food. Avoid touching food directly with your hands.
- Avoid taking more than you can eat. You can always go back for seconds.
- Step away from the buffet if you need to cough or sneeze.
- While in the buffet line, do not eat from your plate.

Fast Food Restaurant Etiquette

The atmosphere at a **fast-food restaurant** is casual, where diners place orders at a counter. After receiving the order, they seat themselves.

- If you do not know what you want to order, do not step up to the counter.
- If there is going to be a wait before you receive your order, step to the side and allow those behind you to order while you wait.
- If you spill something, tell the staff right away.
- Use only the number of napkins and condiments, such as ketchup, you need.

Full-Service Restaurant Etiquette

A **full-service restaurant** offers a lunch menu, a full dinner menu, and full-course meals. A waitstaff serves the guests while they are seated.

- Follow the host to the table.
- After being seated, look at the menu and make your selection.
- Be polite to the server. Say "please" and "thank you" as you order.
- After ordering, place your napkin in your lap and use it when needed.
- Say "thank you" to the server when they serve your food or refill your beverage.
- Wait until everyone at the table is served before eating.
- Stay in your seat and out of the path between tables.
- If you are paying for the meal or chipping in for the cost, leave a tip for the server if you received good service.

Restaurants offer a wide variety of food choices and dining options, making it easier for everyone to find something to enjoy. Sharing meals at home or in a restaurant can strengthen friendships and family relationships.

Name: ______________________________ Date: ____________________

Knowledge Check

Matching

_____ 1. buffet dining
_____ 2. serving utensils
_____ 3. restaurant
_____ 4. waitstaff
_____ 5. condiments

a. a place where people pay to sit and eat meals that are cooked by someone else
b. waiters or waitresses who wait on tables
c. a substance used to add flavor to food
d. diners serve themselves
e tools used to transfer food from a serving dish to individual plates

Multiple Choice

6. Guests are served by waitstaff at a
   a. drive through.
   b. buffet restaurant.
   c. fast food restaurant.
   d. full-service restaurant.

7. When eating at a full-service restaurant
   a. you can go back for seconds.
   b. step away from the buffet if you need to cough.
   c. use serving utensils to get your food.
   d. wait until everyone at the table has been served before eating.

Did You Know?

The oldest fast-food restaurant chain in the United States is White Castle.

Constructed Response

8. Explain what the dining options are in the three types of restaurants. Use details from the reading selection to support your answer.

____
____
____
____
____
____

Name: ______________________________ Date: ____________________

Knowledge Builder

Ordering from a Menu

Directions: No matter what the restaurant, when you order food, you are having a conversation. Study the menu, pick your order, and then complete the conversation activity below as the customer.

Restaurant Menu

The restaurant **menu** is a list of dishes and beverages offered for sale. Most menus are organized into categories. Menu categories include:

- **Appetizers:** a small serving of food before the main course
- **Entrees:** the main course or main part of the meal
- **Sides:** food that accompanies the main course
- **Desserts:** sweet treats to order after the main meal
- **Beverages:** drinks available for purchase

Menu

Appetizers

Tortilla Chips with Salsa	7.49
Buffalo Wings	8.99
Stuffed Mushrooms	5.59

Entrees

All entrees are served with a salad and baked potato or fries.

Fried Chicken	13.59
Sirloin Steak	16.99
Barbeque Ribs	14.99

Desserts

Chocolate Cake	7.99
Apple Pie	6.49
Ice Cream	2.99

Beverages

Soda	3.99
Juice	3.99
Coffee	2.99

Waiter	**Customer**
Hello, I will be your server today.	
Would you like anything to drink?	
Would you like to start with an appetizer?	
And what would you like for the main course?	
What type of dressing would you like for your salad?	
Baked potato or fries?	
What would you like for dessert?	

Cell Phones

Cell phones make it easy for people to stay connected. This technology enables us to stay in contact with those we love from any distance. When speaking on your cell phone, proper etiquette is just as important as when you speak with someone in person. Like in-person interactions, good phone etiquette creates a positive, lasting impression.

Tips for Cell Phone Use

1. Turn your phone to vibrate in public places, such as schools, restaurants, and movie theaters.
2. Pay attention to signs posted about cell phone use. Most public buildings have their own rules about cell phone use.
3. Avoid using your phone while driving, walking, or participating in activities that require your full attention.
4. Call 911 only in the event of an emergency, such as a fire, an accident with injuries, when an ambulance is needed, or to report a crime in progress.
5. Avoid disclosing personal information, such as your age or address, to callers you do not know.
6. Avoid discussing personal problems in public places.

Tips for Answering the Phone

1. Answer the phone within three rings.
2. Give a polite greeting. Example: "Hello, this is (your name). Can I help you?"
3. Speak clearly, but not too loudly, especially if you are in public.
4. If possible, move to an area where your call will not disturb others.
5. Don't overshare information.
6. Be polite. Example: If you can't hear the speaker, say, "Can you please repeat that?" or "Sorry, I'm having trouble hearing you."

Tips for Making a Call

1. Confirm the number before making the call.
2. Introduce yourself. Example: "Hello, this is (name). Is (name) there?"
3. If the call goes to voice message, leave your name, the purpose of your call, and your cell phone number.
4. Wait for your turn to speak. Avoid interrupting.
5. End the call with a polite goodbye.
6. Avoid calling during dinner hour or after 9 PM.
7. Apologize if you get the wrong number.

Cell phone etiquette is important because you will need it for the rest of your life. Phone communication is the basis of many jobs and daily tasks you will encounter.

Name: ______________________________ Date: ______________________

Knowledge Check

Matching

_____ 1. etiquette

_____ 2. interactions

_____ 3. interrupt

_____ 4. disclosing

_____ 5. apologize

a. revealing

b. a set of rules for how to behave

c. ask for forgiveness

d. exchanges

e. stop someone else from speaking

Multiple Choice

6. Call 911 only in the event of
   - a. a celebration.
   - b. an emergency.
   - c. a missing phone number.
   - d. a lost pet.
7. A voice message
   - a. allows callers to leave a photo.
   - b. allows callers to leave a polite goodbye.
   - c. allows callers to leave a written message.
   - d. allows callers to leave a recorded message.

Did You Know?

The first commercially available portable handheld cell phone was 9-inches tall, weighed 2.5 pounds, had 30 minutes of battery life, and sold for $4,000.

Constructed Response

8. Explain why it is important to learn and practice cell phone etiquette. Use details from the selection to support your answer.

____

____

____

____

____

____

____

Name: ______________________ Date: ______________________

Knowledge Builder

Cell Phone Etiquette

Directions: Create an etiquette flyer that a retail store could give to each first-time cell phone owner. Fill in the phones with five important "Do's" and "Don'ts" that all cell phone users should know before purchasing a cell phone.

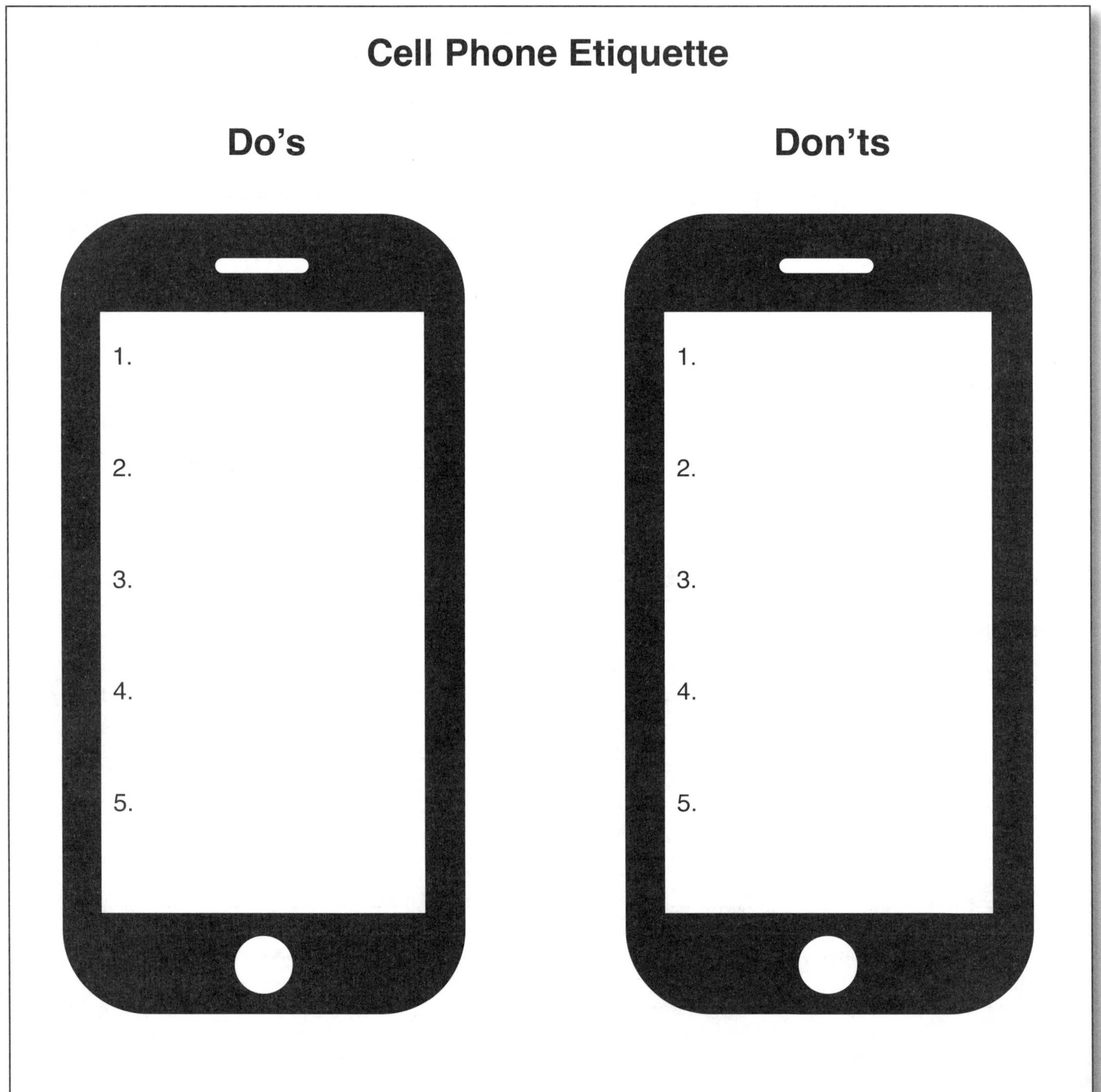

Cell Phone Netiquette

Netiquette is a word that is a combination of the words *network* and *etiquette.* It refers to the polite and correct way of using the internet and behaving online. It is a set of guidelines for online behavior that promotes respect among users and internet safety.

A cell phone is not the same as the internet, but it can access it. The **internet** is a global computer network, while a cell phone is a device that can connect to this network. Cell phones provide a wide range of internet access capabilities. Users can browse websites, use apps, send and receive emails, stream videos and music, and engage in online gaming.

Cell Phone Netiquette Rules

Netiquette rules make the internet a safer and more friendly space. Many people may feel anonymous online, leading them to behave poorly. However, it is important to remember that once you send photos and text messages on the internet, they are there for the rest of the world to see, forever.

Basic Netiquette Rules

1. The golden rule of netiquette is: treat others online as you would like to be treated yourself. This means to use respectful language. Avoid name-calling, cursing, and offensive opinions.
2. Don't send or post pictures you wouldn't want the world to see.

Do's and Don'ts for Online Safety	
Do	**Don't**
• Do tell your parents if you ever get a call or message that makes you uncomfortable. • Do make sure all your social media is set to private so only your friends can see what you post.	• Don't communicate with strangers. • Don't share your passwords, address, or phone number. • Don't share where you go to school, where your parents work, or any other personal information. • Don't agree to meet someone you don't know in real life.

Using proper netiquette is important for your own sake as well as for the well-being of others. Your online activities leave a digital footprint. Information shared online may be saved and shared by others, even if you delete it later. Being careful about what you text, post, or share helps maintain control over your digital presence.

Name: ______________________________ Date: ____________________

Knowledge Check

Matching

_____ 1. netiquette
_____ 2. communication
_____ 3. cell phone
_____ 4. anonymous
_____ 5. online

a. a device that connects to the internet
b. unknown
c. guidelines for online behavior
d. the internet
e. sharing thoughts, ideas, and feelings with others

Multiple Choice

6. What is the Golden Rule of Netiquette?
   a. Use proper grammar and punctuation.
   b. Don't communicate with strangers.
   c. Treat others as you would like to be treated.
   d. Maintain control over your digital presence.
7. What is a digital footprint?
   a. information that exists on the internet as a result of online activity
   b. being careful about what you text, post, or share
   c. communication with strangers
   d. makes your message more readable

Did You Know?

The symbol "@" has become widely recognized today, especially in email addresses. However, this was not always the case. In the past, "@" was chosen for use in email addresses because it was one of the least commonly used symbols on the keyboard.

Constructed Response

8. Explain why it is important to be careful about what you text, post, or share online. Use details from the selection to support your answer.

____

____

____

____

____

____

Name: ______________________________ Date: ____________________

Knowledge Builder

Friendly Netiquette Tips

Directions: Complete the poster with cell phone netiquette tips for internet users.

Civility at School

The primary purpose of school is to educate and prepare students for a successful future. Civility in school promotes education by allowing all students to focus on learning. **Civility** simply means being respectful and treating others as you hope to be treated.

Key Elements of School Civility

When attending school or school events, students are expected to follow school rules, including those for conduct, dress code, and use of electronic devices. Additionally, students should behave in a way that ensures they don't disrupt learning or create unsafe situations. Key elements of school civility include:

- Demonstrate good manners by using appropriate language and behavior.
- Think about how your actions might affect others.
- Listen to others' opinions, ideas, and feelings, even when you disagree.

The School Lunchroom

In the school lunchroom, good manners include respecting others, using polite language, and following the school's lunchroom rules. Waiting patiently in line, welcoming others to the table, staying seated while eating, and cleaning up are just a few good manners we can use in the lunchroom to make mealtime enjoyable for all.

Sportsmanship

Sportsmanship is when students who are playing or watching a sporting event treat each other with respect. This includes respecting teammates, opponents, coaches, and officials, avoiding negativity, and celebrating wins and gracefully accepting losses. It is also important for students to follow the specific rules of the sport and the event's venue.

Bullying

A **bully** is someone who purposely tries to hurt others. They want attention. Sometimes they want to impress their friends, sometimes it is because they enjoy feeling powerful, and sometimes it is because they are being bullied at school or at home by someone else. Bullying includes three areas. **Physical contact** includes such things as pushing, shoving, pinching, hitting, and spitting. **Property damage** can include vandalizing lockers and destroying school supplies. Bullying **social behavior** includes name-calling, spreading rumors, and excluding students from events or study groups.

It takes everyone to stop bullying at school. If you are being bullied, tell someone you trust, such as your parents, teacher, or principal. Avoid areas where the bully may feel comfortable picking on you. Try surrounding yourself with friends or people who will stand up for you. If you see someone who is being bullied, don't stand around and watch. Find someone to help—a friend, teacher, or principal.

Name: ______________________________ Date: ____________________

Knowledge Check

Matching

______	1. civility	a.	a person who purposely tries to hurt someone else
______	2. sportsmanship	b.	being respectful
______	3. bully	c.	how someone behaves within a group
______	4. social behavior	d.	to deliberately damage property
______	5. vandalize	e.	behaving fairly and respectfully in sports

Multiple Choice

6. Lunchroom rules are to help make lunch time
   a. easier for the school staff.
   b. enjoyable for everyone.
   c. go faster.
   d. busy for everyone until class time.

7. The purpose of education is to
   a. give students something to do during the day.
   b. promote respectful behavior.
   c. prepare students for a successful future.
   d. provide fun sports events for the community.

Did You Know?

The National School Lunch Program began in 1946. It has served over 225 billion lunches to school-age children.

Constructed Response

8. Explain why it is important to show civility at school sporting events. Use details from the selection to support your answer.

____

____

____

____

____

____

____

Name: ______________________________ Date: ______________________

Knowledge Builder

Anti-Bullying

Directions: Work with your group to complete the Anti-Bullying Activity. Cut out the ten cards. Each student in the group selects one of the cards. They are to read the bullying problem in the group and explain how they might deal with the situation. The group can discuss other solutions.

Someone repeatedly calls you names.	**Someone makes fun of your shoes.**
Someone spreads a mean rumor about you.	**Someone makes fun of your skin color.**
Someone repeatedly pushes you in the lunch line.	**Someone repeatedly spits on you.**
Someone wants to fight you after school.	**Someone vandalizes your locker.**
Someone threatens to physically hurt you.	**You see someone being bullied.**

Classroom Decorum

Classroom decorum is the polite behavior expected of students in a classroom. It's about using good manners, showing respect, and acting in a way that's considered appropriate for school.

Guidelines for Classroom Behavior

Proper classroom decorum helps create a respectful, attentive, and positive environment, which is important for learning. Guidelines for behavior are essential for creating a classroom where everyone feels safe, valued, and comfortable.

Raise Your Hand for Permission to Speak

Common Classroom Rules:

- **Be Respectful:** Treat classmates, teachers, and school staff with kindness and respect. Bullying, name-calling, or engaging in hurtful behavior is not allowed.
- **Follow Directions:** Pay attention when the teacher is speaking and follow instructions.
- **Raise Your Hand:** Wait your turn and raise your hand when you want to ask a question or share an answer.
- **Stay Seated:** Remain seated unless you have permission to get up. This helps minimize distractions.
- **Be Prepared:** Bring all the materials you need, including books, assignments, and any required tools, to class.
- **Work Quietly:** Work quietly without disturbing others. If you need help, raise your hand.
- **Keep Your Hands and Feet to Yourself:** Respect others' personal space and avoid physical contact unless it's part of a group activity.
- **Clean Up:** Always clean up your desk and the area around you before leaving the classroom.
- **Working in Small Groups:** Respect the work and suggestions of group members. Speak to members in a low voice.
- **Student Presentations:** Be respectful by sitting quietly and keeping your eyes and attention focused on the speaker. Don't distract the speaker.
- **Test Taking:** Remain quiet until everyone is finished.

Consequences of Breaking Classroom Rules

Classroom rules create an environment that makes learning enjoyable. Schools have consequences for those who choose to break the rules. These consequences help students understand how their actions affect other students and encourage them to make better choices in the future. Common consequences for breaking classroom rules include verbal warnings, loss of privileges, detentions, and in some cases, suspension or expulsion.

Name: ______________________________ Date: ______________

Knowledge Check

Matching

_____	1. decorum	a.	how someone acts
_____	2. appropriate	b.	watching and listening
_____	3. behavior	c.	suitable
_____	4. attentive	d.	proper and polite behavior
_____	5. consequences	e.	results of something you do

Multiple Choice

6. When the teacher is speaking, students are expected to

   a. ask questions.
   b. get comfortable.
   c. bring the assignment to class.
   d. sit quietly and pay attention.

7. When you have a question

   a. raise your hand and wait to be called on.
   b. don't distract the speaker.
   c. follow instructions.
   d. work quietly without disturbing others.

Did You Know?

The Boston Latin School in Massachusetts is the oldest public school in the United States. It opened in 1635.

Constructed Response

8. Explain the importance of classroom decorum. Use details from the selection to support your answer.

____

____

____

____

____

____

____

Name: ______________________ Date: ______________

Knowledge Builder

Classroom Rules

Directions: Use the template below to create a colorful handout that your teacher can give to new students. The handout should list five important classroom rules.

CLASSROOM RULES

1.

2.

3.

4.

5.

Writing a Friendly Letter

Friendly letters are typically written to people we know, such as relatives and friends. They resemble a casual, one-on-one conversation with someone where everyday topics are discussed, personal news is shared, and questions are asked.

Five Parts of a Friendly Letter

1. **Heading:** This section includes the sender's address and the date the letter was written. Capitalize the street name, city, and state. Use a comma to separate the city and the state. Although an address is often included, it's not always necessary, especially if the recipient already knows how to contact you. When writing the date, capitalize the month and place a comma between the day and the year.
2. **Greeting:** This states who the letter is addressed to, using the recipient's name. Address the recipient in a friendly way, such as "Dear [Name]," or "Hello [Name],". Capitalize the greeting and the recipient's name.
3. **Body:** This is where the writer conveys their main message, shares news, asks questions, and generally engages in conversation with the recipient. The body can consist of one or more paragraphs: indent each paragraph, capitalize each sentence, and use punctuation at the end of every sentence.
4. **Closing:** This is a friendly way to end the letter. Typical closings include "Sincerely," "Yours truly," or "Love,". Capitalize the first word of the closing and end it with a comma.
5. **Signature:** This is where the sender signs their name using cursive handwriting, usually below the closing. The sender's name is capitalized.

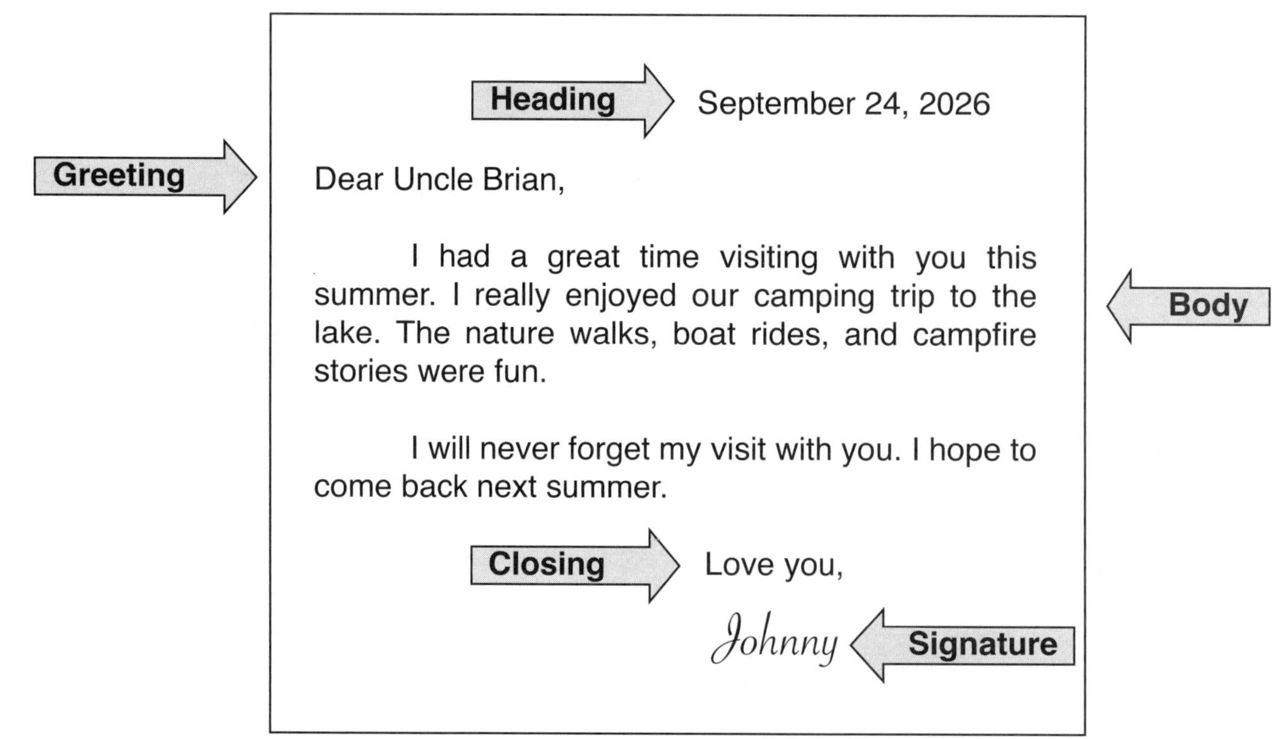

September 24, 2026

Dear Uncle Brian,

I had a great time visiting with you this summer. I really enjoyed our camping trip to the lake. The nature walks, boat rides, and campfire stories were fun.

I will never forget my visit with you. I hope to come back next summer.

Love you,

Johnny

Name: ______________________________ Date: ____________________

Knowledge Check

Matching

_____ 1. sender
_____ 2. recipient
_____ 3. punctuation
_____ 4. signature
_____ 5. indent

a. receiver of a letter
b. symbols used in writing
c. a written name
d. a little space put at the beginning of the paragraph
e. writer of a letter

Multiple Choice

6. What part of a friendly letter is considered the main message?
   a. closing
   b. heading
   c. body
   d. greeting
7. The closing of a letter is a friendly way to
   a. start a letter.
   b. sign your name.
   c. shares thoughts with family and friends.
   d. end a letter.

Did You Know?

The ancient Babylonians created the first envelopes. They were made of clay, folded around the clay tablet that was the letter, and then baked to create a hard shell.

Constructed Response

8. With tools like FaceTime®, phone calls, emails, and texts, why do people still write letters? Use details from the selection to support your answer.

____
____
____
____
____
____
____

Name: ______________________ Date: ______________________

Knowledge Builder

Write a Friendly Letter

Directions: Choose one of the ideas below to write a friendly letter. Write your letter using the stationery template. Remember to indent each paragraph and to use correct spelling and punctuation.

- Write a thank-you letter expressing appreciation for something a person did for you.
- Write a letter to a family member about one of your favorite memories with them.
- Write a letter to a friend sharing your favorite sport, song, movie, or book.

Online Correspondence

Online correspondence is a way to communicate by exchanging messages electronically. Just as letters were once the primary method of written communication, online correspondence serves the same purpose today. It enables individuals to communicate, share information, and build relationships from a distance.

Corresponding Online

Online correspondence includes communicating through email, messaging apps, and chat forums.

- **Email:** transmission of digital messages over a computer network, usually the internet. It provides a quick method for sending and receiving messages, documents, and files to multiple recipients.
- **Social Media:** users can share various types of content, including text, images, videos, and other multimedia.
- **Message Board:** an online discussion platform that allows people to have conversations by posting messages.
- **Chat Room:** instant, interactive conversations, allowing users to communicate with each other in real-time. It's like a live conversation.

Online Correspondence Netiquette

As more of our communications shift online, there is an increasing need for specific guidelines regarding online behavior. Online communication has its own set of rules, which are referred to as **netiquette**, a made-up word that combines the words *network* and *etiquette*. Basic netiquette rules for corresponding on the internet include:

1. Be polite and always communicate respectfully.
2. Be honest, truthful, and do not spread rumors.
3. Avoid sharing your address, phone number, or any other personal information that could put you at risk.
4. Always engage in discussions with respect for others' viewpoints.
5. Remember that most of what you post online can remain there for a long time.
6. Do not share inappropriate or offensive material.
7. Never forward personal emails or photos without the consent of those involved. Always obtain permission before sharing information about another person.

Name: ______________________________ Date: ____________________

Knowledge Check

Matching

_____ 1. online	a.	sharing thoughts, ideas, and feelings with others
_____ 2. correspondence	b.	private
_____ 3. communication	c.	being connected to the internet
_____ 4. netiquette	d.	written communication
_____ 5. personal	e.	guidelines for polite and respectful online behavior

Multiple Choice

6. Before sharing information about another person on the internet
   a. post a picture of the person.
   b. get the person's email address.
   c. check spelling and grammar.
   d. obtain the person's permission.

7. An online message board is a way for people to
   a. have a conversation by posting messages.
   b. send documents and files.
   c. communicate with people in real-time.
   d. have a live conversation.

Did You Know?

In 1995, fewer than 1% of the Earth's population had internet access. Today, more than 66% of the global population actively uses the internet, making it an incredibly accessible communication tool.

Constructed Response

8. Explain how online correspondence has changed the way people communicate. Use details from the selection to support your answer.

____

____

____

____

____

____

____

Name: ______________________________ Date: ____________________

Knowledge Builder

Classroom Message Board

Directions: Create an interactive message board using one of the classroom bulletin boards. Change the discussion topics weekly.

Step 1: Read the message board topic ideas. Choose a topic for the message board.

- What is something a lot of people don't know about you?
- What's the funniest word you know?
- What are five words you think best describe you?
- What makes you a good friend?
- If you could go anywhere in the world on holiday, where would you go?
- What are you good at?
- What is the hardest thing you have ever had to do?
- What things make you happy?
- If you could change your name, what would your new name be?
- What is the best book you have ever read?

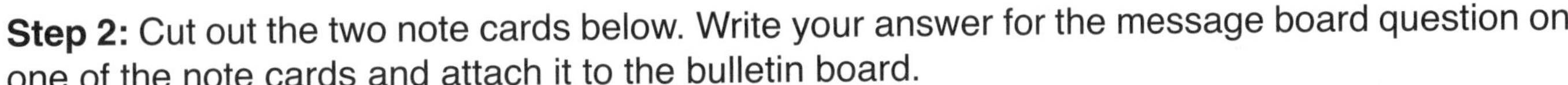

Step 2: Cut out the two note cards below. Write your answer for the message board question on one of the note cards and attach it to the bulletin board.

Step 3: Read other students' answers. Use the other note card to write a comment for one of the posts.

House Rules

Manners are important not only at school or with friends but also at home. It's good to use basic manners everywhere, including within your family. The guidelines for behavior established by your family are often called "house rules."

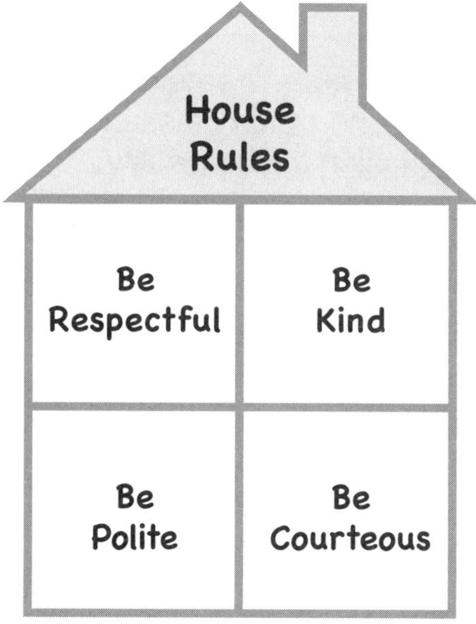

House Rules

Parents set rules for acceptable behavior in the home. Following the house rules will help foster respect within the family. House rules may include:

1. **Polite Words:** Be mindful of how others feel by using polite words such as "please" and "thank you." If you make a mistake or accidentally hurt someone, say "I'm sorry" or "I apologize." Using polite language shows that you are kind, considerate, and aware of others' feelings.
2. **Communication:** Be open to understanding others' opinions. Speak respectfully to family members and listen when they are speaking, avoiding interruptions. This promotes healthy communication within the family.
3. **Table Manners:** Practice good manners while eating by keeping your elbows off the table and your feet on the floor, using utensils properly, and avoiding talking with your mouth full. After the meal, carry your plate to the kitchen sink or dishwasher. Remember to express your appreciation for the meal. Family meals are an opportunity to enjoy each other's company, and good table manners help create a pleasant atmosphere for everyone.
4. **Privacy and Property:** Respect the privacy and property of family members, which allows everyone to have their own space and recognizes their right to privacy. Do not enter a room with a closed door without knocking, eavesdrop on private conversations, or read private materials that are not meant for you. Always ask for permission before borrowing something from others. Respecting privacy helps build trust and respect within the family.
5. **Curfew:** If your parents have given you a certain time to be home, respect that time. Your parents have set this time to ensure that you are home safe so they don't have to worry about you.

It is important to remember that your parents go to work every day to provide you with the food, clothing, and the place you live. Following the rules they have established is a way to show them you appreciate the things they have given you. These rules can help you get along better at home and minimize conflicts. When you are older and have your own home, you will have the opportunity to set your own rules.

Name: ______________________ Date: ______________

Knowledge Check

Matching

_____ 1. house rules
_____ 2. appreciation
_____ 3. privacy
_____ 4. permission
_____ 5. curfew

a. free from being observed or disturbed by other people
b. guidelines for what is acceptable and unacceptable behavior within the home
c. consent
d. gratitude
e. time limit

Multiple Choice

6. Following the house rules
   a. shows that you are aware of others' needs.
   b. is an opportunity to set your own rules.
   c. helps build respect within the family.
   d. is important at school and with friends.

7. Using polite words shows family members you are
   a. listening attentively when others are speaking.
   b. respectful of their privacy and property.
   c. enjoying their company.
   d. aware of others' feelings.

Did You Know?

In 1922, Emily Post published her first book on good manners. It offered more than 600 pages of rules and standards for proper behavior.

Constructed Response

8. Explain the importance of following your family's house rules. Use details from the reading selection to support your answer.

____
____
____
____
____
____
____

Name: ______________________________ Date: ____________________

Knowledge Builder

My Family's House Rules

Directions: Complete the activity below. Write five of your family's rules, then answer the question.

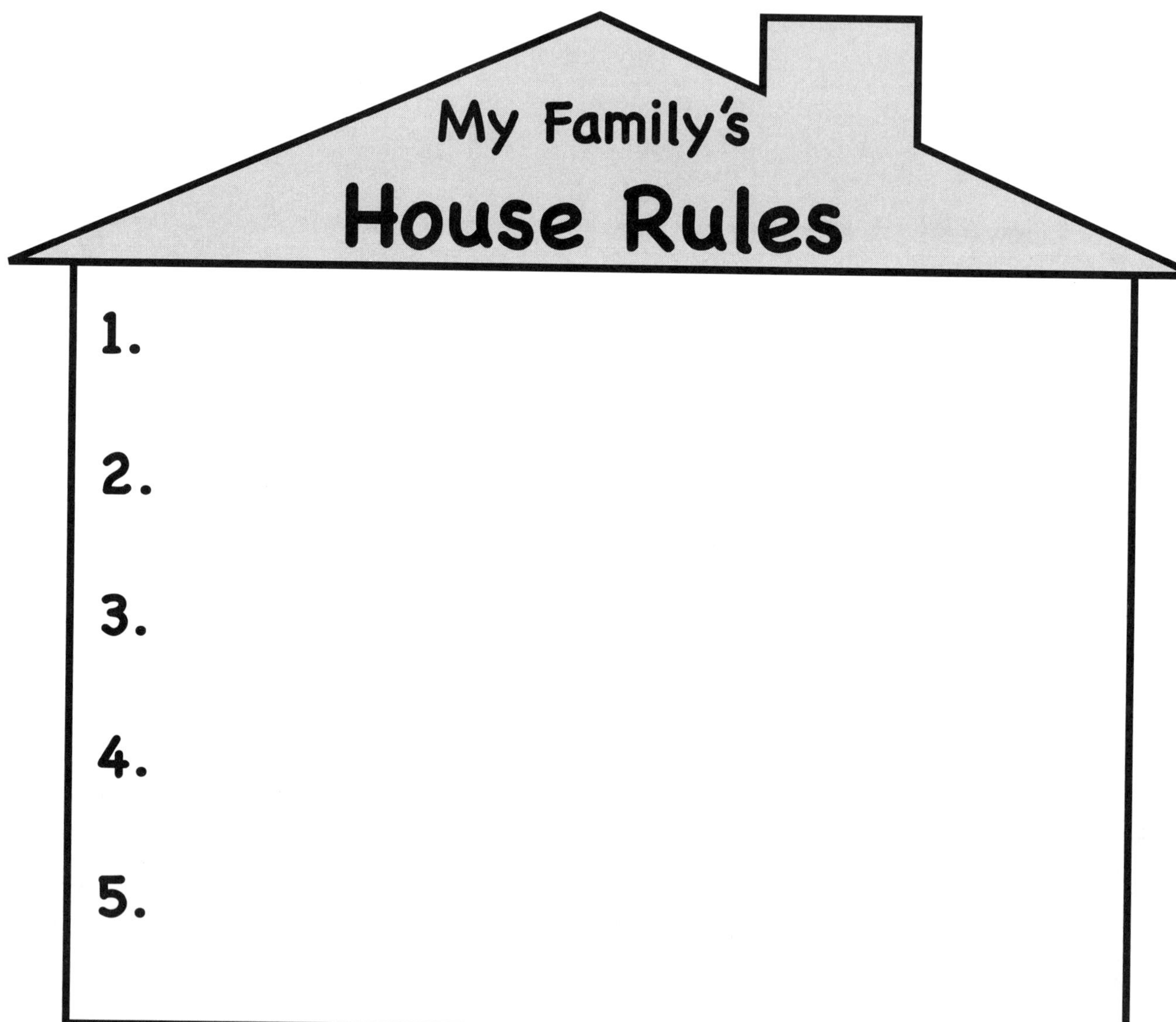

What is a rule you think should be added to your family's house rules? Why?

____

____

____

____

Family Bathroom

In most households, all members share a family bathroom. Parents set the rules for its use. By following these rules, you can help create a comfortable and respectful experience for everyone in your home.

Bathroom Etiquette Is Important

Following the house rules for the bathroom, even if they are different from those in other homes, helps foster respect within the family. Bathroom rules usually focus on privacy, consideration, and cleanliness.

- Bathrooms are private spaces. Always close and lock the door when using the toilet or shower to maintain your privacy. Always knock on the door before entering, even if you believe it's unoccupied. If the door is locked, assume that someone is using the bathroom and wait until it is unlocked.
- Avoid using someone else's personal care products without permission.

- Bathrooms are places where consideration for others is important. Showing thoughtfulness for the next person who needs to use the bathroom is essential. Leaving the area as you found it—or even cleaner—is a key part of bathroom etiquette. This includes wiping up spills, replacing the toilet paper roll, and disposing of waste properly. Be sure to put towels and other items back in their designated places.
- To prevent unpleasant odors, use air fresheners or spray. If available, turn on the bathroom fan to help ventilate the space and reduce any unwanted smells.

- Keeping the family bathroom or bathrooms clean is essential for the health and well-being of everyone in the household. Always make sure to clean up any mess you may have made before leaving. Wipe up spills, splashes, or any other messes. Remember to flush the toilet after use, and if necessary, use the toilet brush to clean it. If needed, clean the toilet seat and lower it afterward. Wash your hands thoroughly with soap and water before leaving the bathroom, as this helps prevent the spread of germs.

By following the family bathroom rules, you can create a pleasant and clean bathroom environment for everyone in your household.

Name: ______________________________ Date: ____________________

Knowledge Check

Matching

_____ 1. household
_____ 2. privacy
_____ 3. consideration
_____ 4. permission
_____ 5. ventilate

a. thinking carefully about how their actions or words might affect other people
b. fresh air to a room
c. approval
d. a family or group of people living together
e. free from being observed or disturbed by other people

Multiple Choice

6. Why is it important to wash your hands after using the bathroom?
   a. keeps the room clean for others
   b. reduces odors
   c. prevents the spread of germs
   d. creates a clean bathroom environment

7. Close and lock the bathroom door when using the shower to
   a. ensure privacy.
   b. avoid leaving unpleasant odors.
   c. help create a comfortable shared space.
   d. keep the room clean.

Did You Know?

Before indoor plumbing became common, outhouses, also known as "necessary houses," were typically located outside the main house.

Constructed Response

8. Explain why following the house rules for sharing a family bathroom is important. Use details from the selection to support your answer.

____
____
____
____
____
____

Name: ______________________________ Date: ______________

Knowledge Builder

Bathroom Doorknob Hanger

Directions: Create a doorknob hanger you can use to communicate with your family when the bathroom is in use. Hotel guests often use doorknob hangers to communicate their needs to hotel staff. Guests hang these on the outside doorknob to convey messages such as "Do Not Disturb," "Maid Service Requested," or "Please Knock."

Steps

1. Decide what you want to say.
2. Print your message on the hanger template.
3. Decorate the hanger using crayons or markers. You could also print and glue clip art from the internet.
4. Cut out the hanger.
5. Cut through the side of the rectangle toward the circle and cut out the circle.
6. To make the hanger more sturdy, glue the paper hanger to a piece of cardboard or thin plastic. Then cut out the hanger again.

Doorknob Hanger Template

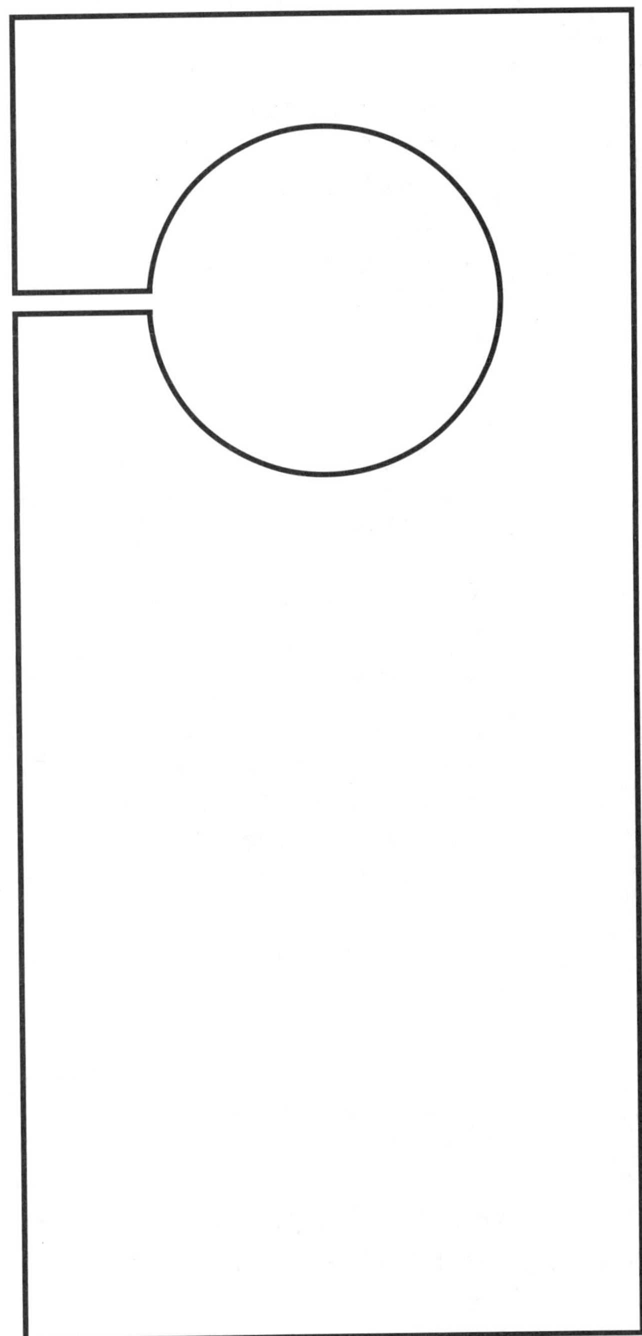

Sharing a Bedroom

Sharing a room allows siblings to build a close relationship by spending more time together. It offers them the chance to share experiences, discuss problems, and learn from one another.

Etiquette for Sharing a Bedroom

Clear guidelines for a shared bedroom create an environment that is both comfortable and respectful. Key areas include personal space, privacy, personal property, noise levels, disagreements, and chores.

- **Personal Space:** Respect your siblings' personal space by treating their space as private and off-limits unless you have explicit permission. Respecting each other's personal space helps minimize arguments and disagreements that can arise from intruding on one another's space.
- **Privacy:** Knock before entering a shared bedroom, particularly if one sibling is changing or getting ready, to avoid awkward or uncomfortable situations.
- **Personal Property:** Ask permission before borrowing or using anything that belongs to a sibling. Taking things without permission can lead to arguments, frustration, and hurt feelings.
- **Noise Levels:** Quiet time is important when sharing a room, especially at night or during study time. Use headphones or earplugs when using personal devices or listening to music. Respecting a roommate's need for quiet during sleep hours or study time fosters a more harmonious living environment.
- **Disagreements:** Work together to resolve disputes peacefully and find solutions that work for both. Discuss any unresolved conflicts with your parents.
- **Chores:** Work with your sibling(s) to keep the room tidy and organized. Clean up messes promptly after activities. Working together to keep the room tidy fosters a sense of shared responsibility.

Sharing a bedroom can be a good experience for siblings, strengthening their bonds and teaching valuable life skills such as sharing and cooperation.

Name: ______________________________ Date: ____________________

Knowledge Check

Matching

_____ 1. sibling

_____ 2. guidelines

_____ 3. minimize

_____ 4. permission

_____ 5. disagreement

a. reduce

b. approval

c. a brother or sister

d. rules

e. dispute

Multiple Choice

6. How can you show respect for your siblings' personal space in a shared bedroom?
   a. Minimize arguments and disagreements.
   b. Use headphones when listening to music.
   c. Treat their space as private and off-limits.
   d. Discuss unresolved conflicts with parents.

7. Why should you knock before entering a shared bedroom?
   a. Shows respect for your roommates' personal space
   b. Fosters a sense of shared responsibility
   c. Strengthens bonds with siblings
   d. Helps avoid awkward situations

Did You Know?

Beds have a surprisingly rich history and fascinating facts surrounding them. For example, the word *mattress* is of Arabic origin, and early beds were often simply cushions placed on the floor.

Constructed Response

8. Explain how sharing a bedroom with a sibling is beneficial. Use details from the selection to support your answer.

____

____

____

____

____

____

Name: ______________________________ Date: ____________________

Knowledge Builder

Etiquette Cube

Directions: Choose four rules for sharing a bedroom that you think are most important. Create a stand-up paper cube to display the rules. Write a rule on each side of the cube. Draw a picture or print artwork from the internet for each side of the cube to illustrate the rule. Decorate each side using colored pencils, crayons, or markers.

Materials:
2 sheets of 8.5 x 11-inch white card stock; glue; colored pencils, crayons, or markers; artwork from the internet (optional)

Step 1: Hamburger fold two sheets of card stock, but fold one of the sheets so that one side is one-half inch shorter than the other side. This makes a flap that extends out one-half inch on one side.

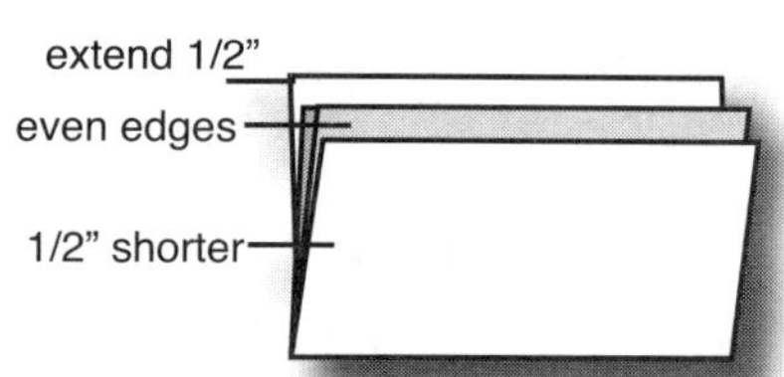

Step 2: Fold the long side over the short side of both sheets, making flaps.

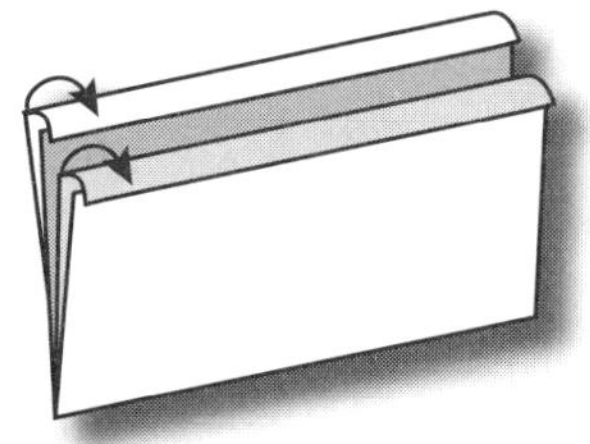

Step 3: Glue along the small folded flap.

Step 4: Place the non-folded edge of the second sheet into the crease and fold the glue-covered flap over this sheet. Do this with the other side.

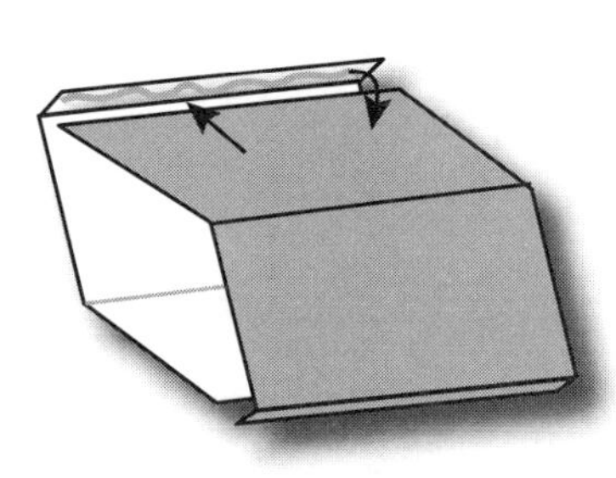

Step 5: The cube can now be collapsed flat to place information and illustrations on all sides.

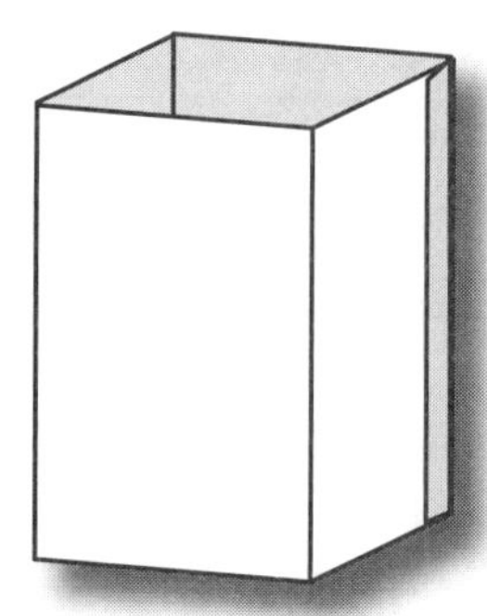

Step 6: Display your cube.

Personal Hygiene

Maintaining **personal hygiene** involves keeping your body clean. Establishing good hygiene habits helps prevent the spread of germs and illnesses, promoting overall health and well-being.

Essential Hygiene Practices

To promote good health, it is important to wash your hands often. Wash your hands before eating, after using the bathroom, after spending time outdoors, or after playing with pets. Handwashing effectively removes dirt and germs to help protect you and those around you from illness.

- **Tips for Handwashing:** (1) Use clean, running water to wet your hands. (2) Apply liquid or bar soap to your hands. Rub your hands together for at least 20 seconds. (3) Scrub the front and back of your hands, between your fingers, and under your nails for a thorough cleaning. (4) Rinse your hands under fresh, running water to remove the soap and germs. (5) Finally, dry your hands with a clean towel.

Caring for your teeth can prevent cavities, bad breath, and other dental problems. Healthy teeth require brushing twice a day and flossing daily.

- **Tips for Brushing Teeth:** (1) Place the toothbrush with toothpaste at a 45-degree angle to the teeth, aiming at the gumline. (2) Brush gently: Use short, back-and-forth motions to cover the top/bottom, front, and back of each tooth. (3) Brush the tongue: Gently brush the tongue to remove bacteria and freshen your breath. (4) Brush for two minutes: Ensure you brush for a total of two minutes. (5) Spit and rinse: Spit out the toothpaste (do not swallow) and rinse with water.

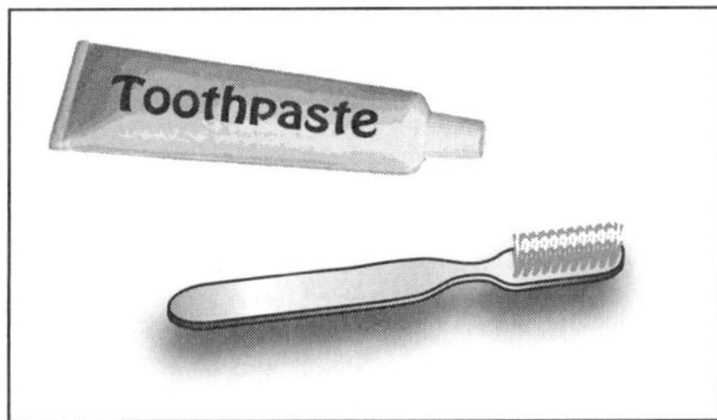

Regular bathing helps keep your body clean and healthy by removing dirt, sweat, and bacteria. It should be included in your bedtime routine or after physical activities.

- **Tips for Bathing:** (1) Wash and carefully dry five key body areas: feet, face, hands, armpits, and bottom. (2) Clean your entire body with soap or body wash at least once a day, paying special attention to areas such as the feet, face, hands, armpits, and bottom. Be sure to scrub under your fingernails and toenails. (3) Use soap or body wash for your skin and shampoo and conditioner for your hair. (4) Dry off completely, then apply deodorant and moisturizer as needed. (5) After bathing, put on clean clothes or pajamas.

Developing and maintaining good personal hygiene habits can benefit you throughout your life.

Name: ________________________________ Date: ____________________

Knowledge Check

Matching

_____ 1. personal
_____ 2. hygiene
_____ 3. flossing
_____ 4. bacteria
_____ 5. habits

a. the practices that maintain cleanliness and promote good health
b. using a special thread (dental floss) to clean between teeth
c. belonging to a particular person
d. something you do often and regularly
e. a type of germ

Multiple Choice

6. Regular bathing or showering helps
   a. protect both you and those around you.
   b. prevent respiratory infections.
   c. keep your skin clean and healthy.
   d. prevent bad breath.
7. Handwashing
   a. should be done twice a day.
   b. removes dirt, viruses, and bacteria.
   c. can help you develop healthy habits.
   d. keeps your skin from becoming dry and flaky.

Did You Know?

In Western Europe during the Middle Ages, frequent full-body bathing was not a common practice, and some people even believed it was unhealthy. During this time, tubs were made of wood.

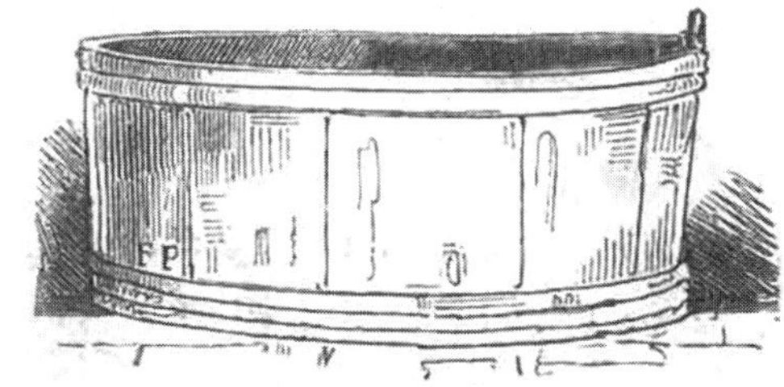

Constructed Response

8. Explain why it is important to practice personal hygiene. Use details from the reading selection to support your answer.

____

____

____

____

____

____

____

Name: ______________________________ Date: ____________________

Knowledge Builder

Handwashing Poster

Directions: Create a step-by-step handwashing poster.

Steps for Creating a Handwashing Poster

1. Write a handwashing tip in each box.
2. Draw or paste pictures in each box to illustrate the tip.
3. Use bright colors and clear text.
4. Share your poster with the class, explaining the importance of each step.

Handwashing Tips		

Bodily Functions and Irritating Habits

Managing bodily functions and irritating habits is essential when interacting with others. It is an important key to creating a positive, respectful, and enjoyable environment for everyone.

Bodily Function Etiquette

Following guidelines for bodily functions is a way to minimize discomfort or offense when with family, friends, and at school.

Coughs and Sneezes

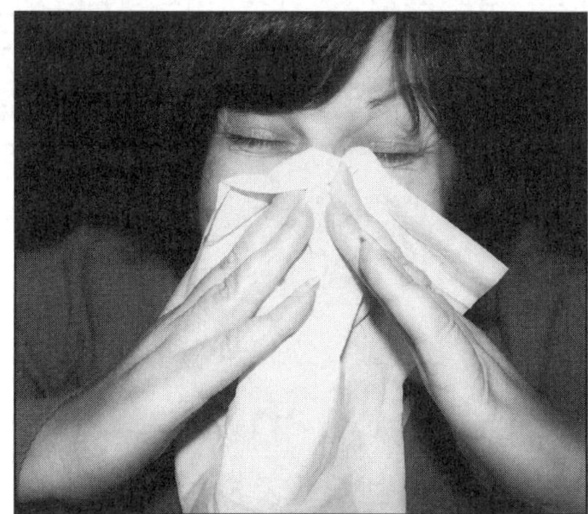

- Coughs and sneezes create respiratory droplets that can become airborne and spread viral infections. To prevent this, cover your mouth and nose with a tissue and turn away from people when you cough or sneeze. Dispose of the used tissues immediately in the trash. Afterwards, wash your hands with soap and water or use an alcohol-based hand sanitizer. If a tissue isn't available, cough or sneeze into your upper sleeve, at the elbow, instead of your hands.

Belching

- If you feel a burp coming, try to cover your mouth with your hand or a napkin to muffle the sound and prevent others from noticing. After burping, it's polite to say, "Excuse me" or "Pardon me."

Irritating Habits

Habits are behaviors that are performed repeatedly. Some habits are irritating and rude.

- **Chewing Gum:** Always chew with your mouth closed to avoid making noises. Avoid blowing bubbles or popping them, as this can be considered immature and disruptive. Have a wrapper or tissue ready to dispose of your gum properly when you're finished.
- **Nose Picking or Blowing:** If you need to clean your nose, do it privately, preferably in a bathroom, and use a tissue or blow your nose instead of picking with your fingers. Afterwards, wash your hands with soap and water or use an alcohol-based hand sanitizer.
- **Nail biting:** Regularly trimming nails can help reduce the temptation to bite them.
- **Spitting:** Avoid spitting whenever possible. If you must spit, turn away from people and spit into a tissue or handkerchief. Dispose of the tissue in the trash. Afterward, wash your hands with soap and water or use an alcohol-based hand sanitizer.

Etiquette is important because it promotes positive interactions at home, school, and in public places. The set of social rules guides behavior, helping individuals navigate social situations with confidence and ease.

Name: ______________________________ Date: ____________________

Knowledge Check

Matching

_____	1. bodily functions	a. unease
_____	2. irritating habits	b. get rid of
_____	3. minimize	c. behaviors that repeatedly cause annoyance in others
_____	4. discomfort	d. activities that occur within the body
_____	5. dispose	e. reduce

Multiple Choice

6. Coughing and sneezing can
   a. spread viral infections.
   b. cause distractions.
   c. frighten people.
   d. cause family members to leave the room.

7. After burping, it is polite to
   a. laugh.
   b. blame someone.
   c. leave the room.
   d. say, "Excuse me."

Did You Know?

In some cultures, belching is a compliment to the cook.

Constructed Response

8. Explain why it is important to follow etiquette guidelines. Use details from the selection to support your answer.

____

____

____

____

____

____

____

Name: ______________________________ Date: ______________________

Knowledge Builder

Sneezing Etiquette Poster

Directions: Create a poster illustrating sneezing etiquette.

Steps:
1. Cut out the Sneezing Etiquette poster and the two hands.
2. Draw a face and hair on the head in the poster.
3. Add some sneezing etiquette tips to the bottom of the poster.
4. Color your drawing and the hands.
5. Cut a tissue in half and glue it to the back side of the paper hands (palm side).
6. Glue the hands to the poster, covering the mouth.
7. Share your poster with the class.

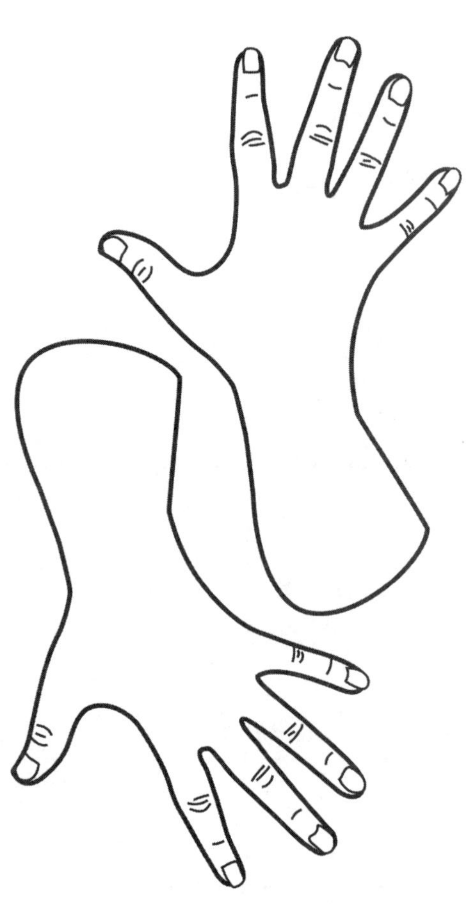

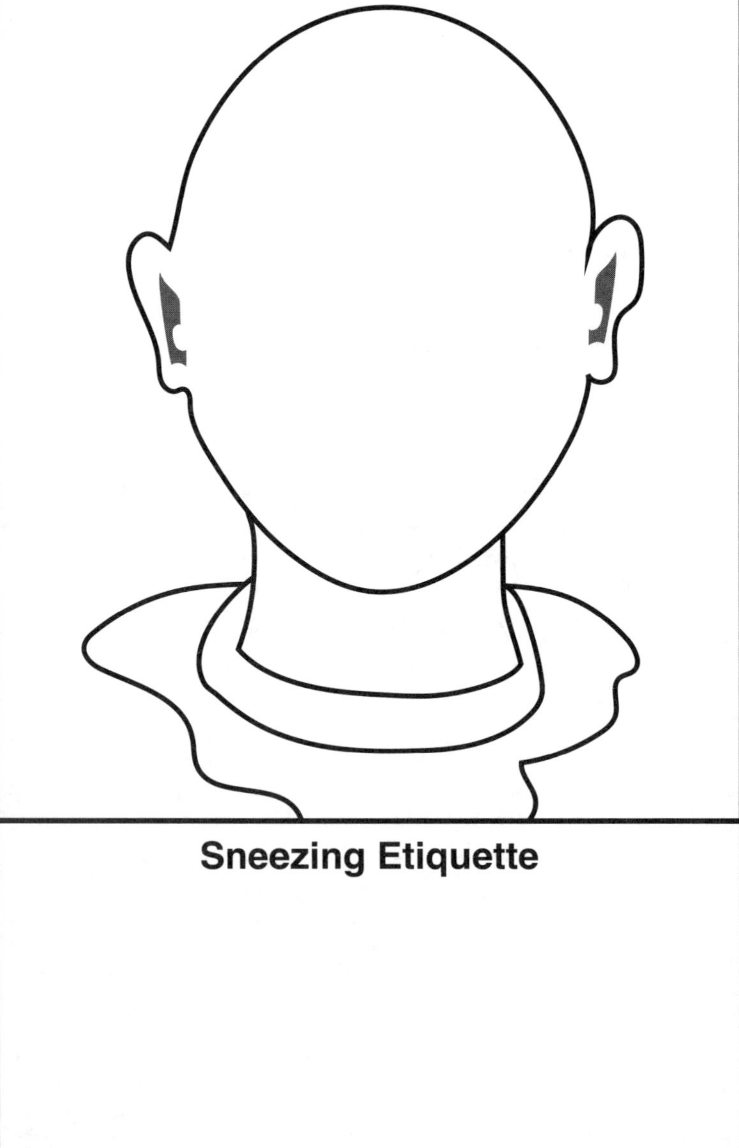

Sneezing Etiquette

Invitations and RSVP Etiquette

Gatherings, especially parties and sleepovers, are excellent opportunities to practice social skills and build friendships. These gatherings encourage everyone to express their thoughts, listen to others, and communicate effectively. Following etiquette guidelines at these events can ensure an enjoyable experience for everyone.

Creating an Invitation

It is important to include specific details when creating an invitation.

- **Host's Name:** Name of the person who is hosting the party.
- **Purpose:** Explain the reason for the celebration. Is it a birthday, sleepover, graduation, or casual get-together?
- **Date and Time:** Include the full date and the start time. Send invitations 2–8 weeks before the event.
- **Location:** Provide the full address of the party location.
- **RSVP Information:** Include an RSVP date (usually 1–4 weeks before the party) and contact details (phone, email, etc.)
- **Details:** Explain how guests should RSVP (phone, email, online) and the deadline for responses.
- **Theme:** If you have a themed party, such as a Halloween Party, mention it in the invitation to help guests plan their outfits or contributions.

Sending Invitations

There are many ways to send invitations. Some people send invitations by mail. Others prefer to use email, social media, or other internet platforms, making it easier to reach guests and track RSVPs.

- **Delivery:** Avoid distributing invitations at school, as it can potentially cause hurt feelings if not everyone is invited.
- **Mail or Email:** Mail invitations or use a digital invitation platform. Avoid distributing invitations during school hours.

RSVP

The term **RSVP** stands for the French phrase "*Répondez s'il vous plaît,*" which means "please respond." An RSVP is a request for you to inform the host whether or not you'll be attending their event so that they can plan accordingly.

- Respond to the invitation, whether accepting or declining.
- Respond by the deadline and in the manner requested in the invitation.

Name: ______________________________ Date: ____________________

Knowledge Check

Matching

_____ 1. host
_____ 2. social skills
_____ 3. invitation
_____ 4. deadline
_____ 5. distribute

a. time or date when something needs to be submitted
b. the person who organizes and welcomes guests to a party
c. the ways people talk, play, and work together
d. friendly request to come to a special occasion
e. deliver

Multiple Choice

6. Why should you avoid passing out invitations at school?
   a. The invitation might get lost.
   b. It could cause hurt feelings if not everyone is invited.
   c. The guest might miss the RSVP deadline.
   d. Guests do not have time to plan for the event.
7. An RSVP is a(n)
   a. explanation of the celebration.
   b. deadline for responses to an invitation.
   c. invitation to a celebration.
   d. request from the host for a response.

Did You Know?

In the Middle Ages, wealthy families would hire monks skilled in calligraphy to handwrite their invitations.

Constructed Response

8. Why are parties an excellent opportunity to practice social skills and build friendships? Use details from the selection to support your answer.

____
____
____
____
____
____

Name: ______________________________ Date: ____________________

Knowledge Builder

Party Invitation

Directions: In the box below, create an invitation to a party.

Steps For Party Invitation

1. **Choosing a Party Theme:** You can select from a variety of themes, such as birthday, Halloween, sleepover, movie night, sports tournaments, or any other idea you prefer.
2. **Designing the Invitation:** Select a design that matches your chosen theme. Utilize paper, markers, crayons, colored pencils, stickers, and other craft supplies to create your invitation. You can either draw a picture or print artwork from the internet to illustrate the invitation.
3. **Essential Information:** Include important details about the event, such as the host's name, the event's purpose, date and time, location, and RSVP information.

Being a Host

Being a good host involves making guests feel welcome and comfortable, and ensuring they have a good time while respecting the host's home and rules. This includes thoughtful planning, fun activities, clear communication, and attention to the guests' needs.

Guidelines for Hosts:

By following these guidelines, teenagers can be effective and considerate hosts, creating a positive and enjoyable experience for their guests.

Before the Party

- Send invitations. The invitation should include the location and the start and end times for the party.
- Tidy up the house, especially areas like the living room, kitchen, and bathrooms.
- Plan for a variety of snacks for the guests.
- Prepare games, music, or other activities planned to keep guests entertained.

During the Party

- Greet all your guests when they arrive. Tell them you are glad they came. Explain where the bathroom is if guests have not been to your home before. If other friends are already there, bring new guests to them so they can get to know each other while you welcome the latest arrivals. If the guest is a new friend, introduce them to the group.
- When all your guests have arrived, join your friends. Explain house rules such as staying within designated areas and respecting the host's property.
- Explain the rules for the party games and activities to your guests. Ensure that everyone is involved. If you notice someone standing alone, especially if they are new to the group, encourage them to participate. Keep an eye on the interactions to make sure all guests are getting along.
- Turn up the lights and play some music to signal the end of the party. Help guests depart and thank them for coming.

After the Party

- Help tidy up the house, put away food and drinks, and clear any used items.
- If appropriate, send a thank-you note or message to guests, especially if they brought a gift or were particularly helpful.
- Discuss with family members about how the party went, what could be improved, and any lessons learned.

Parties create an opportunity for friends to connect and meet new people. They are a fun way to celebrate, enjoy music, dance, and play games. Being a good host ensures that everyone enjoys attending your parties.

Name: ______________________________ Date: ____________________

Knowledge Check

Matching

_____ 1. host
_____ 2. designated
_____ 3. opportunity
_____ 4. communication
_____ 5. connect

a. sharing information with others
b. building a relationship with someone
c. a specific place that's set aside for a particular purpose
d. the person who organizes and welcomes guests to a party
e. chance

Multiple Choice

6. When a guest brings a gift, a host should
   a. present the guest with a gift.
   b. send the guest a thank-you note or message.
   c. share the gift with other guests.
   d. open the gift after the party.

7. What should a host do if someone is not participating in the party games?
   a. Do not invite the person to the next party.
   b. Bring it to the attention of the other guests.
   c. Do not allow them to participate in other games.
   d. Encourage them to participate.

Did You Know?

In ancient Rome, public birthday celebrations were held for emperors, the founding dates of cities and temples, and the gods associated with particular days. Roman men and women had private birthday celebrations, which included gifts, guests, and food.

Constructed Response

8. Explain what being a good host involves. Use details from the selection to support your answer.

____

____

____

____

____

____

Name: ______________________________ Date: ______________________

Knowledge Builder

Tri-Fold Brochure

Directions: Create a foldable brochure to guide students on hosting a successful party. Examine a variety of brochures. Look closely at how graphics, text, and print features enhance the information presented in the brochure. Use information from the reading selection to create your brochure. Utilize paper, markers, crayons, colored pencils, stickers, and other craft supplies to create your brochure. You can either draw a picture or print artwork from the internet to decorate the six panels.

Tri-Fold Brochure Instructions

The tri-fold brochure is a single sheet of heavy paper with information and pictures printed on both sides and folded into three equal sections.

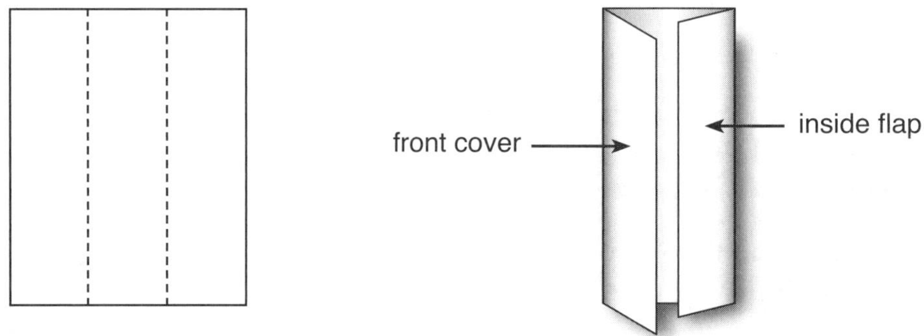

After folding, there are six panels for information (three panels on the outside and three panels on the inside).

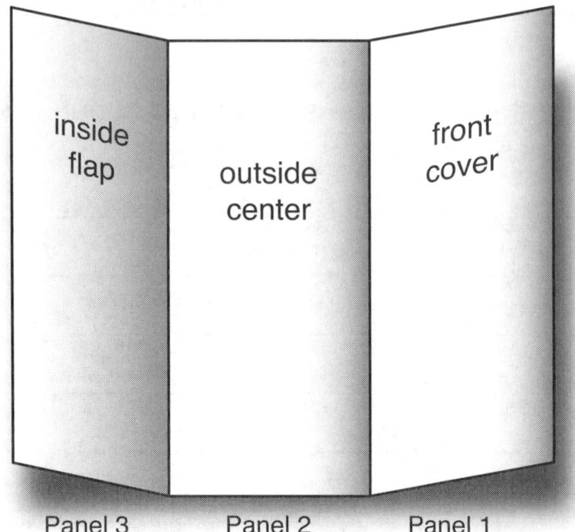

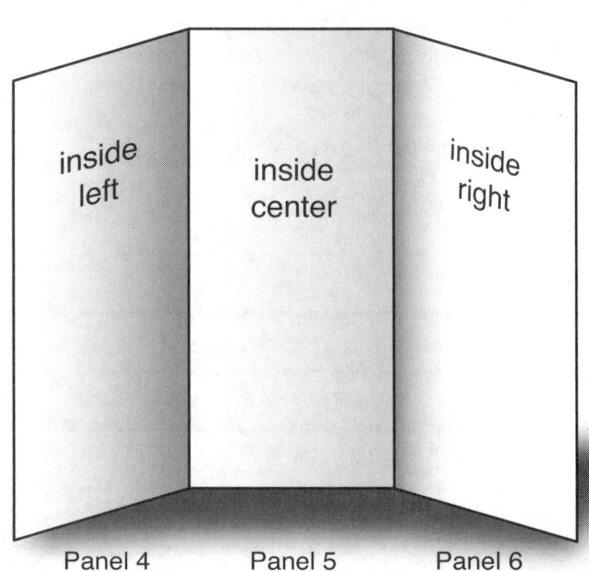

Being a Great Guest

When attending a party, it is important to demonstrate thoughtful and respectful behavior. Remember, you are a guest in someone's home.

Etiquette Guidelines

Being a good guest involves being polite, helpful, and respectful of the host's home and rules. By following party guidelines, you can help create an enjoyable experience for everyone at the party.

__Before the Party__

Replying to a party invitation helps the host with planning.

- Let the host know if you're coming or not as soon as possible.
- Arrive on time. Notify the host if you will be late.

__During the Party__

You can be a great guest by following party etiquette.

- Be polite. Remember to say "please" and "thank you" and address the host and their family members respectfully.
- Offer to help with meal preparation, cleaning up, or other tasks.
- Follow the house rules. If the host has set any guidelines, such as noise levels or areas that are off-limits, respect them.
- Participate in games, dancing, or whatever is planned. If you notice someone standing alone, invite them to join the group or conversation.

__After the Party__

It is important to remember that the host and their parents put a great deal of effort into the party. Show your appreciation for the effort and the invitation.

- Thank the host and the host's parents for their hospitality when you leave their home. Within a week or two, send a thank-you note, email, or text message to show your appreciation.
- Tidy up the space you used for the party. Leave the home tidy.
- Offer to help with any final cleaning or packing.

Parties are fun celebrations. They are excellent opportunities to build friendships and make lasting memories. However, guests should follow the rules of etiquette to ensure the experience is enjoyable for everyone.

Name: ______________________________ Date: ____________________

Knowledge Check

Matching

_____ 1. demonstrate
_____ 2. appreciation
_____ 3. host
_____ 4. etiquette
_____ 5. house rules

a. behaviors to use in social situations
b. guidelines for what is acceptable and unacceptable behavior within a home
c. person who invites people to a party
d. show
e. being thankful

Multiple Choice

6. Why is it important to reply to party invitations?
   a. It's an opportunity to build friendships.
   b. It helps the host plan the party.
   c. It shows thoughtful and respectful behavior.
   d. It creates a fun party for everyone.
7. What should you do if someone is not participating in the party games or activities?
   a. Tell the person to go home.
   b. Ignore the person.
   c. Remember to say "please" and "thank you."
   d. Invite the person to join the activity.

Did You Know?

August is the most popular month for birthday parties.

January	February
March	April
May	June
July	August
September	October
November	December

Constructed Response

8. Explain how to be a great guest. Use details from the selection to support your answer.

____
____
____
____
____
____
____

Name: ____________________ Date: ____________________

Knowledge Builder

Etiquette Puzzle

Directions: Create a guest etiquette puzzle.

Materials		
card stock paper	colored pencils	pencil
markers	scissors	plastic baggie

Steps

Step 1: Choose nine etiquette rules for guests you want to use for your puzzle.
Step 2: Either copy this page on card stock or glue the puzzle outline to the card stock.
Step 3: Use a colored pencil or marker to write a rule in each puzzle piece.
Step 4: Decorate the entire cardstock with colored pencils or markers.
Step 5: Cut out the puzzle pieces and store them in a plastic baggie.
Step 6: Share your puzzle with classmates for them to put together.

The United States Flag

The American flag is an important national symbol of the United States. It serves as a reminder of the nation's dedication to freedom, justice, and unity for all its citizens.

History of the American Flag

On July 4, 1776, the 13 British colonies of America declared their independence from Great Britain. These colonies eventually became the original 13 states of the United States. In 1777, a law was enacted to establish an official flag for the new nation.

Features of the American Flag

The design of the American flag reflects the history of the United States. The 13 stripes stand for the 13 original colonies. The 50 stars stand for the 50 states. A star is added to the flag when a new state joins the United States. The United States Congress adopted the current 50-star version in 1960 after Hawaii became a state.

The number of stars on the flag has changed as more states have joined the nation, but the colors and their meanings remain the same. Each of the colors on the flag has a meaning:

- **Red:** valor and bravery
- **White:** purity and innocence
- **Blue:** vigilance, perseverance, and justice

Proper Etiquette for Reciting The Pledge of Allegiance

When reciting "The Pledge of Allegiance," you are making a promise of loyalty to the United States.

> **The Pledge of Allegiance**
>
> "I pledge allegiance to the Flag of the United States of America, and to the Republic for which it stands, one Nation under God, indivisible, with liberty and justice for all."

Guidelines for the Pledge of Allegiance

- Stand up and face the flag.
- Boys and men remove hats, if wearing one.
- Place your right hand over your heart.
- Recite the pledge, then sit down.

Proper Etiquette for Displaying the United States Flag

- Fly the flag from sunrise to sunset, unless it's illuminated at night.
- Don't let the flag touch the ground.
- When displayed with other flags, the U.S. flag should be at the highest point.

Name: ______________________ Date: ______________________

Knowledge Check

Matching

_____ 1. symbol
_____ 2. Congress
_____ 3. valor
_____ 4. pledge
_____ 5. allegiance

a. promise
b. something that represents something else
c. bravery
d. a team of elected officials who make the laws
e. loyalty

Multiple Choice

6. The stars on the United States flag represent the 50
   a. Civil War heroes.
   b. presidents.
   c. states.
   d. American Revolutionary battles.
7. When displayed with other flags, the U.S. flag should be
   a. to the left of the other flags.
   b. at the bottom of the line of flags.
   c. at the highest point.
   d. to the right of the other flags.

Did You Know?

Someone who designs flags is a vexillographer, and the art of flag design is called vexillography!

Constructed Response

8. Explain the importance of the United States flag. Use details from the selection to support your answer.

____
____
____
____
____
____
____

Name: ________________________________ Date: ____________________

Knowledge Builder

My Flag

Directions: Create a flag.

Steps

1. Choose something important in your life as the theme for your flag: family members, pets, friends, favorite sports, or after-school activities.
2. Research the meanings of different colors.
3. Draw your flag design using symbols that are meaningful to you and colors that represent your theme.
4. Share your flag with the classroom.

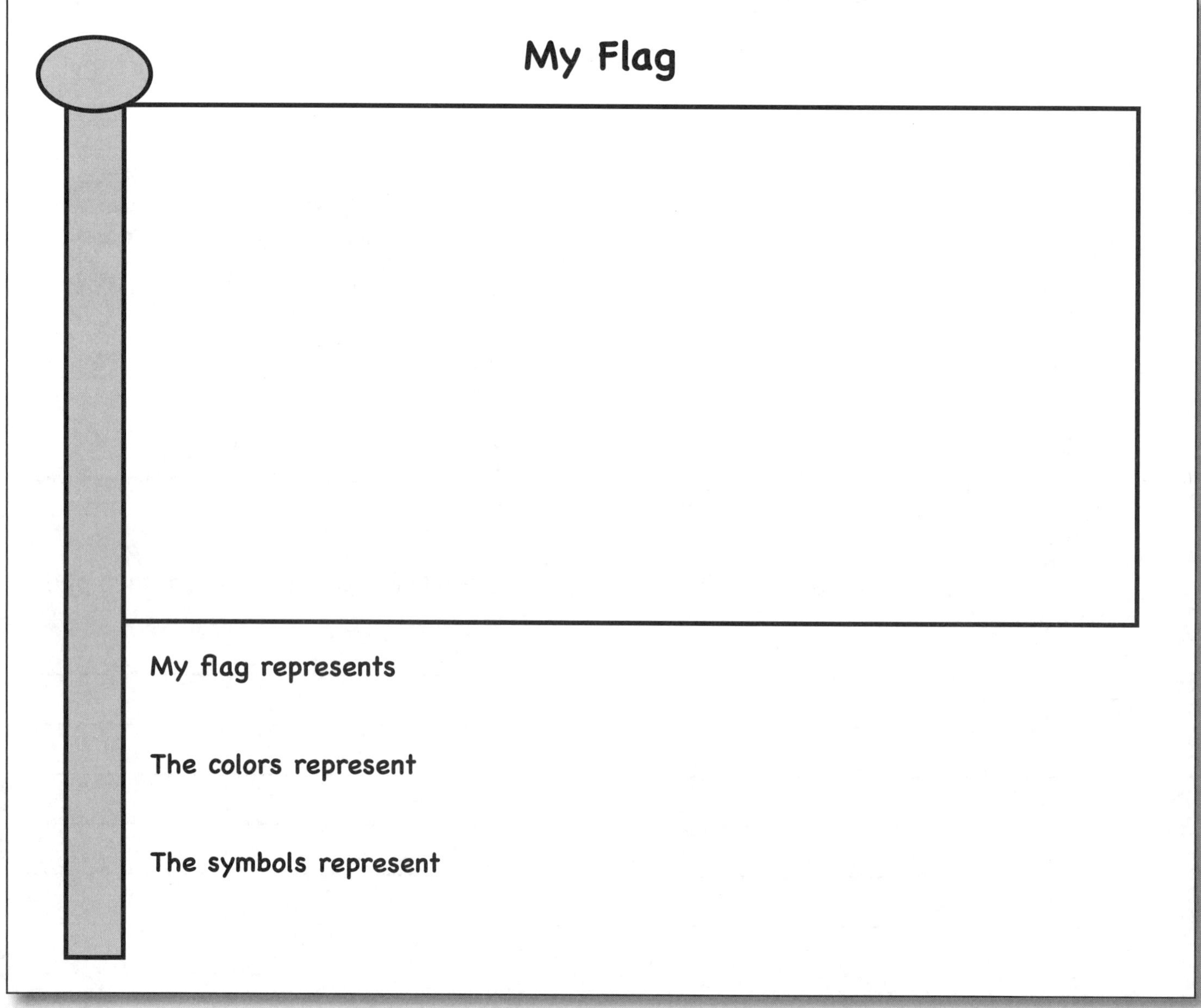

The National Anthem

Almost every country in the world has a national anthem. An **anthem** is a special song that helps people feel connected to their nation and remember its history and values. These songs are often played at important events, like official ceremonies or sports games.

The Star-Spangled Banner

"The Star-Spangled Banner" is the national anthem of the United States. It was initially written as a poem and consisted of four verses. In 1814, Francis Scott Key was inspired to write it after he witnessed the American flag still flying over Fort McHenry during the War of 1812.

The poem was later set to music. The song gained popularity, and President Woodrow Wilson signed an executive order in 1916 designating it as "the national anthem of the United States" for all military ceremonies. On March 3, 1931, Congress formally designated "The Star-Spangled Banner" as the national anthem of the United States.

The Star-Spangled Banner
Verse One

O say can you see, by the dawn's early light,
What so proudly we hailed at the twilight's last gleaming,
Whose broad stripes and bright stars through the perilous fight,
O'er the ramparts we watched, were so gallantly streaming?
And the rockets' red glare, the bombs bursting in air,
Gave proof through the night that our flag was still there;
O say does that star-spangled banner yet wave
O'er the land of the free and the home of the brave?

National Anthem Etiquette

Proper etiquette during the playing of the national anthem demonstrates respect for the nation and its history. It's a way to show patriotism and honor those who have served in the military or sacrificed for the country. Basic etiquette for the "National Anthem" includes:

- Face the flag if it is displayed. If the flag is not displayed, face the source of the music.
- If wearing a hat or any other head covering, it should be removed and held in the right hand.
- Place your right hand over your heart.
- It's important to be quiet and respectful during the anthem; avoiding talking, eating, or other distractions.

Name: ______________________________ Date: ____________________

Knowledge Check

Matching

_____ 1. anthem
_____ 2. designate
_____ 3. executive order
_____ 4. ceremony
_____ 5. national

a. special instruction that the president of the United States gives to the government
b. a special song that helps people remember the history of their nation
c. a way of celebrating important events
d. something that relates to the whole country
e. appoint

Multiple Choice

6. The "Star-Spangled Banner" is the national anthem for which country?
   a. Great Britain
   b. United States
   c. Canada
   d. Mexico
7. Standing during the National Anthem shows
   a. respect for those who served in the military.
   b. respect for your grandparents.
   c. respect for the end of wars.
   d. respect for the president.

Did You Know?

A newspaper first printed Francis Scott Key's poem that became our national anthem under the title "Defence of Fort M'Henry." Later, a music store printed the patriotic song with sheet music for the first time under the title "The Star-Spangled Banner."

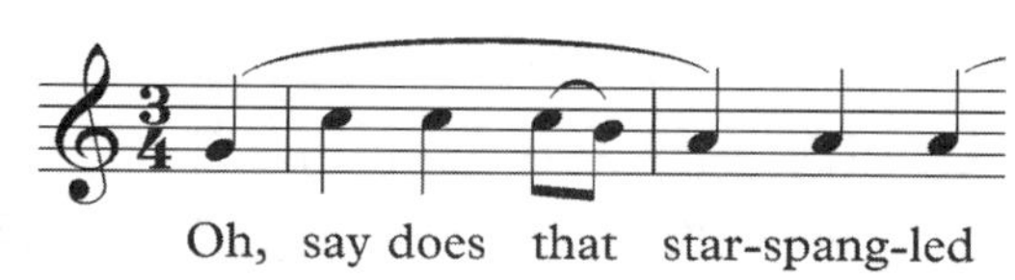

Constructed Response

8. Explain why it is important to use proper etiquette when the National Anthem is played. Use details from the selection to support your answer.

____
____
____
____
____
____

Name: ______________________ Date: ______________

Knowledge Builder

News Article

Directions: Write an article for the school newspaper. Research the history of the United States National Anthem. Fill in the blanks below with the research. Use the information to write the article on a separate sheet of paper or use a computer to type and print the article.

Headline: (a short attention-getting phrase that presents the main idea of the article)

____

Byline: (your name) ______________________________

Lead Paragraph: (All the important information is revealed in the opening paragraph.)

Who: ______________________________

What: ______________________________

When: ______________________________

Where: ______________________________

Why: ______________________________

How: ______________________________

Explanation: (supporting details, quotes, examples, and interesting facts)

Conclusion: (wraps up the article and makes the story stick in the mind of the reader)

Respecting Veterans

Veterans Day and Memorial Day are recognized as national holidays in the United States, dedicated to honoring the men and women who have served in the U.S. military. On these two holidays, most government offices, including the post office, are closed.

Memorial Day

Memorial Day is a time to honor the men and women who have died while serving our country, both in times of peace and war. Originally called Decoration Day, the day was first established to commemorate the 620,000 soldiers who lost their lives during the Civil War. In 1971, Congress declared Memorial Day a federal holiday. It is observed on the last Monday in May.

Honoring Veterans

1. The U.S. flag should be flown at half-staff from dawn till noon on Memorial Day.
2. Attend a Memorial Day parade or observance.
3. Attend a cemetery's Memorial Day ceremony and place flowers at the graves.
4. Wear a red poppy. Red poppies symbolize the blood shed during wartime. Artificial ones are made and handed out to raise money for veterans' causes. Wear one to remember the fallen and commemorate the sacrifice they made for our country.

Veterans Day

Veterans Day is a special holiday that was first celebrated as Armistice Day. It was established to honor the end of World War I on November 11, 1918. In 1954, Armistice Day was officially renamed Veterans Day. Today, it is a day set aside to honor all American veterans, regardless of the conflicts in which they served. It is celebrated with parades, ceremonies, and expressions of gratitude to veterans. Each year, a special ceremony is held at Arlington National Cemetery in honor of veterans.

Honoring Veterans

1. Say "Thank you for your service" or "We appreciate your sacrifice" when you meet a veteran.
2. Create and send thank-you cards, letters, or artwork to veterans.
3. Take the time to learn about a veteran's experiences by listening to their stories.

Celebrating Memorial Day and Veterans Day is a way of saying "Thank you" to the millions of veterans who have sacrificed for the safety and freedoms of the United States.

Name: ______________________________ Date: ______________________

Knowledge Check

Matching

_____ 1. veteran
_____ 2. memorial
_____ 3. commemorate
_____ 4. Armistice Day
_____ 5. federal holiday

a. something created to honor and remember a person, event, or group of people
b. the end of World War I
c. designated day off each year recognized by the United States government
d. someone who has served in the armed forces
e. remember and honor a person or event from the past

Multiple Choice

6. Veterans Day is a holiday to
   a. honor the United States government.
   b. honor all American veterans.
   c. honor the men and women who have died while serving our country.
   d. honor the United States Navy.
7. Memorial Day is a holiday to
   a. honor those who have died serving our country.
   b. honor all American veterans.
   c. honor all United States presidents.
   d. honor the end of the Civil War.

Did You Know?

There are 11 U.S. federal holidays. These are days that the U.S. federal government recognizes as holidays, and federal employees are typically given the day off with pay.

Constructed Response

8. Explain why it is important to show respect for our veterans. Use details from the selection to support your answer.

____

____

____

____

____

____

Name: ______________________ Date: ______________

Knowledge Builder

Veteran Exhibit

Directions: Conduct an interview with a veteran. Use the information to create an exhibit. Share the exhibit with the classroom and display it on Veterans Day.

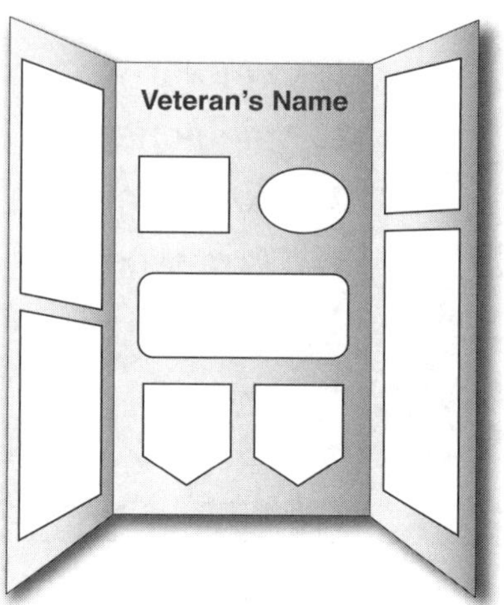

An exhibit is a visual method for communicating information. To create your exhibit, gather data from your research, interviews, photos, and online images. Present the information on a display board, which typically consists of three sections and is made of cardboard. Your exhibit should be neat, attractive, easy to read, colorful, and organized in a logical order.

Exhibit Ideas

Veteran's Name:

Military Branch:

Years Served:

Enlistment and Training:

Wars or Campaigns Served In:

Military Life:

Rank:

Medals:

Coming Home:

Interesting Facts:

Name: ______________________ Date: ______________________

Knowledge Builder

Basic Interview Tips

1. **Request an Interview:** Contact the person to be interviewed and explain who you are, why you want to talk to them, and what you wish to find out. Find out the branch of the service they were in and their job. Set a time to conduct the interview.
2. **Research:** Research the branch of service of the veteran and the time period served. Use the information to prepare specific questions for the interview.
3. **Interview Day:** Bring a pencil, notebook, and interview questions. Obtain permission to take pictures of the veteran for use in your display.
4. **Conduct the Interview:** Maintain eye contact when asking questions. Don't interrupt. Listen carefully to the answers given. Don't be afraid to ask follow-up questions.
5. **End Interview:** Thank the veteran and leave your school contact information.

Interview Questions

Enlistment and Training:

How old were you when you joined the military?

What made you decide to join the military?

Life in the Military:

Where were you stationed?

What was your job or assignment?

Did you see combat?

Name: ______________________ Date: ______________________

Knowledge Builder

Interview Questions (cont.)

What was your favorite part of serving?

What was the most surprising thing about military life?

Coming Home and Afterwards:

Did you go back to school or work?

How did your service change you?

What are some lessons you learned from your service?

Other Questions:

Name: ______________________ Date: ______________________

Knowledge Builder Rubric

Components	Advanced 4	Proficient 3	Nearing Proficient 2	Below Proficient 1
Directions	All project directions were followed.	Most project directions were followed.	Some project directions were followed.	None of the project directions were followed.
Effort	The project shows a significant amount of time spent and very careful, neat work.	The project shows a good amount of time spent and careful and neat work.	The project shows some amount of time spent and is slightly lacking in neatness.	The project shows a minimal amount of time spent and is not well-organized.
Appearance	The project makes excellent use of color and graphics.	The project makes good use of color and graphics.	The project makes some use of color and graphics.	The project has minimal use of color and graphics.
Language and Mechanics	The project contains correct spelling, capitalization, punctuation, and grammar.	The project contains a few errors in spelling, capitalization, punctuation, and/or grammar.	The project contains careless or distracting mistakes in spelling, capitalization, punctuation, and/or grammar.	The project contains many errors in spelling, capitalization, punctuation, and/or grammar.

Teacher Comments:

Answer Keys

Constructed Response answers will vary, but suggested answers have been included.

Unit 1: Etiquette

Etiquette vs. Manners

Knowledge Check (page 3)

Matching

1. d 2. b 3. c 4. e
5. a

Multiple Choice

6. c 7. a

Constructed Response

8. Learning proper etiquette and good manners gives you the essential skills for a happy and successful life.

Knowledge Builder (page 4)

Across

2. conduct 6. courteous
8. appropriate 9. polite
10. attitude

Down

1. manners 3. decorum
4. etiquette 5. honesty
7. civility

Unit 2: Social Interactions

Introductions

Knowledge Check (page 6)

Matching

1. d 2. e 3. c 4. a
5. b

Multiple Choice

6. c 7. b

Constructed Response

8. Learning to give and receive introductions is important. Introductions are a way to show respect. It is a way to help people feel comfortable and part of a group.

Knowledge Builder (page 7)

Teacher check

Making Conversation

Knowledge Check (page 9)

Matching

1. b 2. e 3. d 4. a
5. c

Multiple Choice

6. c 7. b

Constructed Response

8. Conversation is how we get to know people and build friendships. Learning and practicing basic conversation skills will make communicating with others easier. Practicing conversation etiquette will make you a better communicator. Developing good conversation skills will help you make friends and develop strong relationships with others.

Knowledge Builder (page 10)

Teacher check

Unit 3: Table Manners

Basic Table Manners

Knowledge Check (page 12)

Matching

1. c 2. d 3. a 4. b
5. e

Multiple Choice

6. c 7. a

Constructed Response

8. Table manners are basic skills that you will use throughout life. Practicing basic table manners can create a pleasant and comfortable eating environment for everyone involved. Knowing how to behave appropriately at the table can improve your confidence in social situations. Using proper table manners keeps mealtime together enjoyable for everyone.

Knowledge Builder (page 13)

Teacher check

Table Setting

Knowledge Check (page 15)

Matching

1. c 2. d 3. a 4. e
5. b

Multiple Choice

6. c 7. b

Constructed Response

8. A properly set table ensures that everything is organized and that everyone has what they need before sitting down to eat.

Knowledge Builder (page 16)

A. Plate – middle of the setting
B. Napkin – to the left of the plate
C. Glass – above the knife and spoon, to the right of the plate
D. Fork – on napkin, to the left of the plate
E. Knife – to the right of the plate
F. Spoon – to the right of the knife

Restaurant Etiquette

Knowledge Check (page 18)

Matching

1. d 2. e 3. a 4. b
5. c

Multiple Choice

6. d 7. d

Constructed Response

8. Restaurants offer a wide variety of dining options. Buffet dining offers a variety of food, and people serve themselves. The atmosphere at a fast-food restaurant is casual, where diners place orders at a counter. After receiving the order, they seat themselves. A full-service restaurant offers a lunch menu, a full dinner menu, and full-course meals. The guests are served by a waitstaff while they are seated.

Knowledge Builder (page 19)

Teacher check

Unit 4: Online Etiquette

Cell Phones

Knowledge Check (page 21)

Matching

1. b 2. d 3. e 4. a
5. c

Multiple Choice

6. b 7. d

Constructed Response

8. Cell phone etiquette is important because you will need it for the rest of your life. Phone communication is the basis of many jobs and daily tasks you will encounter.

Knowledge Builder (page 22)

Teacher check

Cell Phone Netiquette

Knowledge Check (page 24)

Matching

1. c 2. e 3. a 4. b
5. d

Multiple Choice

6. c 7. a

Constructed Response

8. Your online activities leave a digital footprint. Information shared online may be saved and shared by others, even if you delete it later. Being careful about what you text, post, or share helps maintain control over your digital presence.

Knowledge Builder (page 25)

Teacher check using the Knowledge Builder Rubric on page 73.

Unit 5: School Etiquette

Civility at School

Knowledge Check (page 27)

Matching

1. b 2. e 3. a 4. c
5. d

Multiple Choice

6. b 7. c

Civility at School (cont.)
Constructed Response
8. Civility ensures students behave in a way that doesn't disrupt the event or create an unsafe situation.

Knowledge Builder (page 28)
Teacher check

Classroom Decorum
Knowledge Check (page 30)
Matching
1. d 2. c 3. a 4. b
5. e
Multiple Choice
6. d 7. a
Constructed Response
8. Following the rules creates an environment where all students feel safe and respected. When someone breaks the rules, there are consequences.

Knowledge Builder (page 31)
Teacher check using the Knowledge Builder Rubric on page 73.

Unit 6: Correspondence Etiquette

Writing a Friendly Letter
Knowledge Check (page 33)
Matching
1. e 2. a 3. b 4. c
5. d
Multiple Choice
6. c 7. d
Constructed Response
8. Friendly letters resemble a casual, one-on-one conversation with someone where everyday topics are discussed, personal news is shared, and questions are asked.

Knowledge Builder (page 34)
Teacher check

Online Correspondence
Knowledge Check (page 36)
Matching
1. c 2. d 3. a 4. e
5. b
Multiple Choice
6. d 7. a
Constructed Response
8. Handwritten letters were once the primary method of written communication; online correspondence serves the same purpose today. Social media, email, chat rooms, and message boards all facilitate quick and immediate communication. These methods allow users to send and receive messages within seconds, enabling real-time or near real-time interactions.

Knowledge Builder (page 37)
Teacher check

Unit 7: Family Etiquette

House Rules
Knowledge Check (page 39)
Matching
1. b 2. d 3. a 4. c
5. e
Multiple Choice
6. c 7. d
Constructed Response
8. Following house rules can help you get along better at home and minimize conflicts. It helps build trust and respect within the family, creates a pleasant atmosphere for everyone, and promotes healthy communication within the family.

Knowledge Builder (page 40)
Teacher check

Family Bathroom
Knowledge Check (page 42)
Matching
1. d 2. e 3. a 4. c
5. b
Multiple Choice
6. c 7. a
Constructed Response
8. By following the family bathroom rules, you can create a pleasant and clean bathroom environment for everyone in your household.

Knowledge Builder (page 43)
Teacher check using the Knowledge Builder Rubric on page 73.

Sharing a Bedroom
Knowledge Check (page 45)
Matching
1. c 2. d 3. a 4. b
5. e
Multiple Choice
6. c 7. d
Constructed Response
8. Sharing a bedroom can be a positive experience for siblings, strengthening their bonds and teaching valuable life skills such as sharing and cooperation.

Knowledge Builder (page 46)
Teacher check using the Knowledge Builder Rubric on page 73.

Unit 8: Hygiene

Personal Hygiene
Knowledge Check (page 48)
Matching
1. c 2. a 3. b 4. e
5. d
Multiple Choice
6. c 7. b
Constructed Response
8. Establishing good hygiene habits helps prevent the spread of germs and illnesses, promoting overall health and well-being.

Knowledge Builder (page 49)
Teacher check using the Knowledge Builder Rubric on page 73.

Bodily Functions and Irritating Habits
Knowledge Check (page 51)
Matching
1. d 2. c 3. e 4. a
5. b
Multiple Choice
6. a 7. d
Constructed Response
8. Etiquette is important because it promotes positive interactions at home, school, and in public places. The set of social rules guides behavior, helping individuals navigate social situations with confidence and ease.

Knowledge Builder (page 52)
Teacher check using the Knowledge Builder Rubric on page 73.

Unit 9: Being a Host or Guest

Invitations and RSVP Etiquette
Knowledge Check (page 54)
Matching
1. b 2. c 3. d 4. a
5. e
Multiple Choice
6. b 7. d
Constructed Response
8. Gatherings, especially parties and sleepovers, are excellent opportunities to practice social skills and build friendships. These gatherings encourage everyone to express their thoughts, listen to others, and communicate effectively.

Knowledge Builder (page 55)
Teacher check using the Knowledge Builder Rubric on page 73.

Being a Host
Knowledge Check (page 57)
Matching
1. d 2. c 3. e 4. a
5. b
Multiple Choice
6. b 7. d
Constructed Response
8. Being a good host involves making guests feel welcome and comfortable, and ensuring they have a good time while respecting the host's home and rules. This includes thoughtful planning, fun activities, clear communication, and attention to the guests' needs.

Knowledge Builder (page 58)
Teacher check using the Knowledge Builder Rubric on page 73.

Being a Great Guest
Knowledge Check (page 60)
Matching
1. d 2. e 3. c 4. a
5. b

Multiple Choice
6. b 7. d

Constructed Response
8. When attending a party, a great guest demonstrates thoughtful and respectful behavior.

Knowledge Builder (page 61)
Teacher check using the Knowledge Builder Rubric on page 73.

Unit 10: Showing Respect

The United States Flag
Knowledge Check (page 63)
Matching
1. b 2. d 3. c 4. a
5. e

Multiple Choice
6. c 7. c

Constructed Response
8. The American flag is an important national symbol of the United States. It serves as a reminder of the nation's dedication to freedom, justice, and unity for all its citizens.

Knowledge Builder (page 64)
Teacher check using the Knowledge Builder Rubric on page 73.

The National Anthem
Knowledge Check (page 66)
Matching
1. b 2. e 3. a 4. c
5. d

Multiple Choice
6. b 7. a

Constructed Response
8. Proper etiquette during the playing of the national anthem demonstrates respect for the nation and its history. It's a way to show patriotism and honor those who have served in the military or sacrificed for the country.

Knowledge Builder (page 67)
Teacher check using the Knowledge Builder Rubric on page 73.

Respecting Veterans
Knowledge Check (page 69)
Matching
1. d 2. a 3. e 4. b
5. c

Multiple Choice
6. b 7. a

Constructed Response
8. Showing respect for veterans is a way of saying "Thank you" to the millions of veterans who have sacrificed for the safety and freedoms of the United States.

Knowledge Builder (page 70–72)
Teacher check using the Knowledge Builder Rubric on page 73.